friendship
bracelets

friendship
bracelets

35 gorgeous projects to
make and give

Lucy Hopping

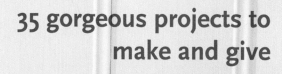

Published in 2014 by CICO Kidz
An imprint of Ryland Peters & Small
519 Broadway, 5th Floor, New York NY 10012
20–21 Jockey's Fields, London WC1R 4BW
www.rylandpeters.com

10 9 8 7 6 5 4 3 2 1

Text copyright © Lucy Hopping 2014
Design, photography, and illustration
copyright © CICO Kidz 2014

A CIP catalog record for this book is
available from the Library of Congress and
the British Library.

ISBN: 978-1-78249-107-1

Printed in China

EDITOR: Katharine Goddard
DESIGNER: Louise Turpin
ILLUSTRATOR: Louise Turpin
PHOTOGRAPHERS: Terry Benson
and Jo Henderson
STYLISTS: Rob Merrett and Sophie Martell

contents

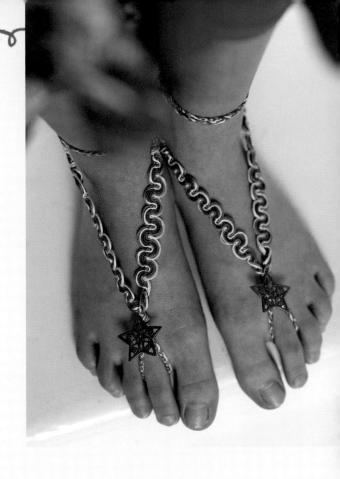

INTRODUCTION

This book features 35 stunning braiding projects with clear step-by-step instructions to help you. Each project has been given a skill level from easy (one flower) to advanced (three flowers) so that you can start with the simpler designs and move onto the more advanced ones as your skills and confidence grow.

Macramé is the main method of making the friendship bracelets in this book. This is a way of knotting threads to create a new fabric. The most popular knots are forward, backward, and square knots that are all fully explained and illustrated along with others in the techniques section (see page 10).

Sailors are thought to have originally started the craft of macramé by adapting the knots they used for daily life on board ship to decorate items, such as knife handles and bottles. Macramé was a very popular craft in Victorian times when ladies would decorate placemats, bedding, and clothes with intricate knotted patterns in very fine threads.

During the 1970s, a resurgence in the popularity of macramé led to the advent of friendship bracelets. These were originally given by one friend to another as a symbol of friendship. According to tradition, a bracelet should be tied onto the wrist of a friend who may make a wish. The bracelet should be worn until it's totally worn-out and falls off by itself, at which point the wish is supposed to come true.

You can choose from four chapters of fun projects in this book. Each one has its own color palette. So Sweet has plenty of pretty pastel colors combined with sequins and rhinestone chain. Tribal Attitude is inspired by native American and African crafts and Boho chic, so we have kept to a natural color palette—brown, orange, cream, turquoise, and natural. Materials include leather, hemp, and wood. Nautical Knots has a neat, simple, and charming style—colors are limited to red, white, and blue with accents of silver and metal to create the seaside feel. Finally, Neon Brights is your time to go wild and experiment with colors and materials—fluorescent colors clash with pompom trim, metal studs, and quirky shoelaces!

introduction

6

However, the great thing about this craft is that you can adapt each design to your own taste—so, for example, take a project from So Sweet and make it in zesty neon shades, and you will create a totally different look. See page 20 for more advice on designing your own braids.

You will soon be creating fantastic bracelets, as well as cuffs, headbands, sandals, and even covering your headphones or making braided bowls to hold all of your new makes!

materials

BRAIDING MATERIALS

EMBROIDERY FLOSS (THREAD)
Made from cotton, embroidery floss is formed from six thin strands. It is the most common material used for friendship braids. Usually sold in 8¾-yd (8-m) hanks and in an array of bright colors, it is ideal for braiding.

PEARL COTTON
Pearl cotton is made out of 100% cotton but is twisted rather than stranded and, therefore, easier to handle as it does not split.

WAXED CORD
This is stiffened cotton, which makes a sturdier braid. The knots can be seen more clearly, which can look great.

SHAMBALLA CORD
A robust nylon thread ideal for creating macramé-style knots. The smooth surface is great for neat knots and sliding knot fastenings.

STRING
A versatile cord, usually made from cotton. It has a smooth finish and is great for making natural-looking styles.

HEMP CORD
Hemp is biodegradable and an eco-friendly alternative to synthetic cording. It usually comes in a natural color. It often has a rough surface that can add texture to a project.

COTTON KNITTING YARN
This is ideal for chunkier braids and projects, such as the crochet braids on page 45. It has a smooth surface.

YARN
Leftover scraps of wool yarn are great for making braids and similar projects. Wool is made from animal fibers, usually sheep, and comes in a variety of thicknesses, from very fine (Laceweight/2-ply) to very thick (Bulky or Chunky). There are also plenty of synthetic yarns available that are bright and colorful. Experiment with fibers and thickness to get the look you want. A chunky bracelet could look really cool!

SHOELACES
Available in a wide selection of colors, thicknesses, and materials, shoelaces can be used to great effect in braids. They tend to fray when cut, so always tape before cutting or ask an adult to burn the ends to seal them.

SILKY FURNISHING CORD
A chunky, silky cord that is ideal for headbands, belts, and other larger projects. It frays easily when cut, so always tape the ends before you cut them! It is available in plenty of colors and thicknesses.

FABRIC
Thin strips of fabric are great to braid with. Jersey or T-shirt material is especially good as it rolls up into tubes and creates neat knots. Printed cottons add pattern and texture to your crafts.

CHAIN

Metal curb chain comes in a wide variety of thicknesses and colors, and adds an edginess to your braids. It can be woven into your braids or stitched on afterward.

LEATHER AND SUEDE CORD

These types of cord are fast becoming very popular braiding materials. They are both available in a wide variety of colors, thicknesses, and shapes. Try using flat or round cord for varying effects. Some varieties come with snakeskin effect or with studs already attached.

EMBELLISHMENTS

BEADS

There are so many shapes, sizes, and material of beads that you are bound to find the right ones for your project! Types of bead include wooden beads, plastic pony beads, glass beads, metal beads, and picture beads.

CHARMS

These are small metal or plastic trinkets that are threaded into or stitched onto your braids. They have a small jump ring, which can be used to thread it into the necessary position. Available in silver, gold, or bronze colored metals, with colored enamel or without, the possibilities are endless!

SEQUINS

Add a touch of sparkle to your braids by using pretty sequins threaded onto your wrapping cords when knotting. Simply thread your cord or floss through the central hole to attach it to your work. They can also be stitched on afterward.

FEATHERS

Responsibly sourced feathers add a bright and fun look to larger braiding projects.

BELLS

They will hear you coming with the tinkle of bells on your braids! Bells come in various sizes and colors. They can be threaded onto your braids in a similar way to beads and sequins.

BUTTONS

Buttons can add color and texture to your braids. They come in a variety of shades, materials, and sizes so you can match them to your projects. As well as layering them, such as in the Button Bracelet on page 113, you could use them as fastenings.

BRASS NUTS

A quirky addition to friendship braids, brass nuts look really on-trend. Buy from hardware stores or raid your dad's tool box. (Ask him first!) They come in a variety of sizes.

STUDS

Studs are a great way of adding a tough look to your bracelets. They come in a variety of sizes, shapes, and colors. The studs we use in this book have sharp prongs on the back of them. Press carefully through the braid and then fold the prongs into the center to fix in place.

RHINESTONE CHAIN

Rhinestone chain is a metal chain studded with small rhinestone gems running along it. It comes in a wide selection of colors, sizes, and widths. It is easy to cut to size with craft scissors. Try stitching it onto finished bracelets, or gluing a chain onto bangles before wrapping them with floss.

materials

9

techniques

BASIC KNOTS

To create most of the projects in this book you need to master only a few basic types of knot. Practice these before you begin making your bracelets. Backward and forward knotting techniques create flat braid designs, such as chevrons, diagonal lines, Peruvian waves, and leaf motifs. You can make your braids wider or narrower depending on the number of threads used. The Josephine knot is a flat and decorative knot, which can be used singularly, as in the nautical knot headband (page 81) or in a row as in the Josephine braids (page 74). The lark's head knot is useful for attaching threads into your braids—check out the dream catcher bracelets (page 56) or the sliding macramé fastening (page 20) to see how helpful a knot it is!

BACKWARD KNOT

1 Hold the left-hand floss tight and wrap the right-hand floss around it. Pull the end through the loop created. Pull the floss to tighten the knot.

2 Repeat to create a double knot—the knot goes from right to left.

HALF-BACKWARD KNOT

1 Follow step 1 only of a backward knot.

FORWARD KNOT

1 Hold the right-hand floss tight and wrap the left-hand floss around it. Pull the end through the loop created. Pull the floss to tighten the knot.

2 Repeat to create a double knot—the knot goes from left to right.

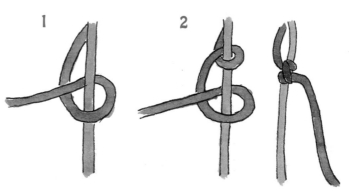

HALF-FORWARD KNOT

1 Follow step 1 only of a forward knot.

JOSEPHINE KNOT

1 Take two pieces of floss and create a loop with one of them. Place the second floss underneath the loop.

2 Wrap the second floss over the first tail of the loop, and then under the second tail of the loop.

3 Finally, wrap it over the loop and underneath itself to complete the knot.

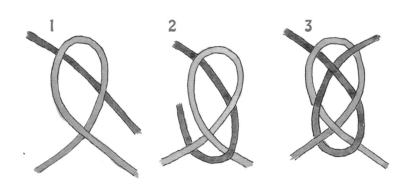

LARK'S HEAD KNOT

1 Fold the cord in half and place the loop under the horizontal floss or item you are tying it to.

2 Reach under the loop and over the horizontal floss and grasp the two loose strands, bringing them down through the loop.

3 Pull and tighten the knot.

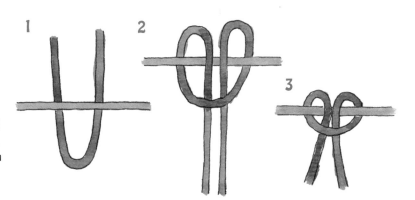

WRAPPED BRAIDS

No knots are needed here! Simply wrap the thread around a central core very tightly and tidily until it is all covered. To secure the wrapping cord, thread it up through the center of the core and trim any excess.

ROUND BRAIDS

"Kumihimo" is the Japanese name for cords made on a braiding wheel, and they were traditionally used by Samurai warriors to lace their armor and kimonos. The threads intertwine as they are passed over each other on the wheel to create a really strong circular braid.

The four-strand braids on page 122 work in a similar way to Kumihimo, but threads are intertwined by hand rather than a wheel so they are a lot thinner. The spiral braids on page 24 also create a round finish. By repeatedly knotting the outer color thread around a central "core," a natural twist occurs in the braid.

THREE-WAY BRAIDS

Braids aren't just for your hair! This is one of the first braiding (plaiting) techniques that many of us learn and it is such a versatile technique that it continues to be popular. Three-way braids are created using three cords that wrap over each other.

THREE-WAY BRAID

1 Label your three bundles of thread or ribbon from left to right as A, B, and C.

2 Start with the left-hand thread (A) and bring it into the center.

3 Now move the right-hand thread (C) into the center.

4 Repeat steps 2 and 3 until your braid is the length you require for your project.

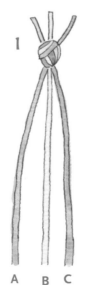

1

A B C

2

B A C

3

B C A

SQUARE BRAIDS

Use the macramé square knot technique to create sturdy, solid braids with squared-off edges. You can alternate the knot to get a smooth, straight braid or keep repeating steps 1 and 2 for a twisted look.

SQUARE KNOT
(FIGURE-OF-FOUR KNOT)

1 Start with three threads: put the base floss in the center and a knotting floss either side. Bring the left knotting floss over the base floss and under the right knotting floss.

2 Now bring the right knotting floss under the base floss and through the loop of the left floss.

3 Repeat in reverse, so the right thread goes over the base thread and left thread goes under.

4 Pull the threads to tighten the knot.

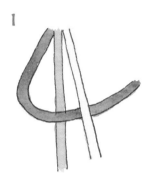

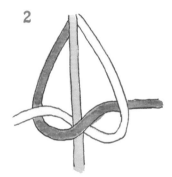

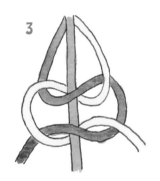

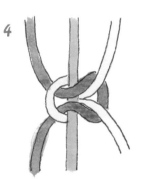

TWISTED BRAIDS

Twisted cords are really simple to make. Attach one end of your cords to a secure surface and hook the other ends around your fingers or a pencil. Twist until the cord is straining to fold up on itself, place the ends together, and let go; the braid should twist itself together. Secure with a knot to hold the twist in position.

CROCHET BRAIDS

Using a crochet hook to make a chain stitch creates a knitted braid. Knitted cords are stretchier than knotted or woven braids and so are ideal if you do not know what size to make a bracelet.

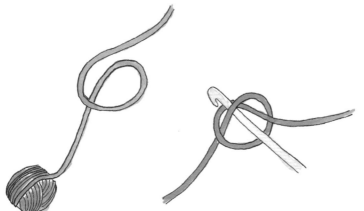

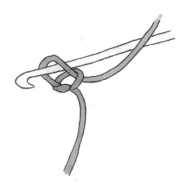

1 Create a loop with the yarn, about 6 in (15 cm) from the free end.

2 Insert the crochet hook through the center of the loop and hook the free end.

3 Pull this strand of yarn through and up onto the working area of the crochet hook. This makes a slipknot.

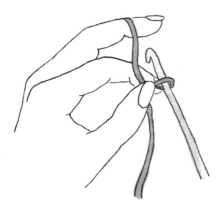

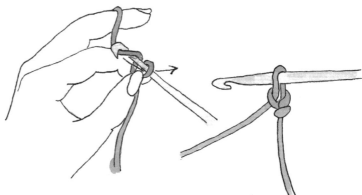

4 Hold the crochet hook, with its slipknot, in your right hand and wrap the yarn around with your left hand. Once you have the yarn wrapped, hold the base of the slipknot with the thumb and index finger of your left hand.

5 Bring the yarn over the crochet hook from back to front and hook it. Draw the hooked yarn through the loop of the slipknot on the hook and up onto the working area of the crochet hook.

6 You have now made one chain stitch. Repeat steps 4–5 to increase the length of your chain as required.

techniques

14

WOVEN BRAIDS

Weaving is an ancient way of making fabrics and we have used it in two very different ways in this book. A "warp" is created on a loom (a simple device that holds the threads taut), and these are threads that run vertically, up and down. Then the "weft" threads are woven over and under the warp threads to create a strong fabric.

USING A CARD LOOM

1 To make your loom, cut small notches approximately $^1/_8$–$^1/_4$ in (2–5-mm) apart from each other at both the top and bottom of a piece of card.

2 Wrap the warp onto the card, placing a thread into each notch, until the warp is the width you want your braid to be. Tie the ends together in a knot to secure.

3. Cut a length of thread for the weft and begin weaving it over and under the warp (see page 65).

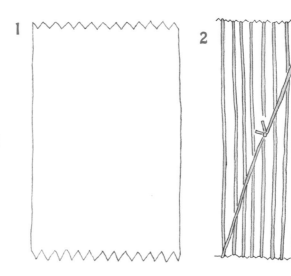

USING A BEADING LOOM

1 Use gridded paper to create your design.

2 Cut your warp threads 18 in (45 cm) long. You will need one more thread than the number of beads in the width. Tie them in a knot at one end and divide the bunch in half. Slip the knot under the nail on one of the spindles, then put each thread into a groove of its own, placing one bunch then the other so that the threads are evenly spaced.

3 Turn the spindle until you have rolled up 6 in (15 cm) and then tighten the wing nut on the side. Pull the threads tight and set carefully in the grooves on the other end of the loom. Tie threads into a knot and slip the knot over the nail on the other spindle. Roll the spindle until the threads are tight.

4 Cut a 24-in (60-cm) long weft thread, tie it to the outer warp thread, and begin weaving it over and under the warp (see page 60).

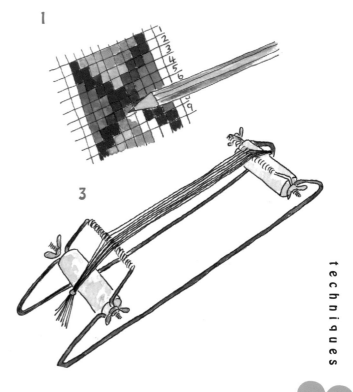

techniques

15

ADDING EMBELLISHMENTS

Many of the projects in this book include embellishments and decorations. They can be added in many different ways and it is explained in each project, but here are some extra tips for when you are designing your own braids.

THREADING EMBELLISHMENTS ONTO BASE CORD

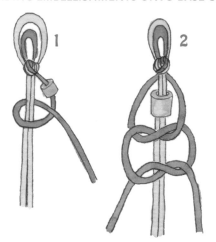

The most common technique for adding beads is to thread the bead onto the cord you are using to make the knot, and then using the knot to secure it in place. However, if you are making a braid with a core of threads, you can thread it on those and knot in place.

ATTACHING STUDS

Arrange the studs along the length of the braid. Press down through to the back and then fold the points inward to fix in place.

ADDING FEATHERS

Feathers can either be woven into your braids or attached afterward using strong glue.

SEWING ON RHINESTONE CHAIN

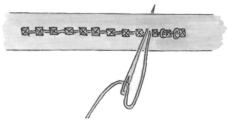

Using scissors, cut your rhinestone chain to size. Then place it on the surface of the braid and, using embroidery floss, secure in place with stitches over each bar between the gems.

CUTTING CHAIN

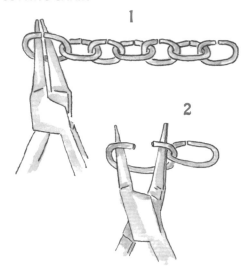

Some chains are thin and made of metal soft enough to be cut to size using scissors. If not, take a small pair of pliers and insert the closed nose into the piece of chain. Open them up and they will stretch open the link. Unhook the chain and you have a shorter piece ready to stitch or use in your project.

HOW TO SECURE YOUR BRAID TO A WORK SURFACE

When braiding, make sure you have a tidy work surface and plenty of space to spread out your floss or cord. Also, your floss must be secured to a surface so when you make your knots they are tight and even. There are different ways to do this.

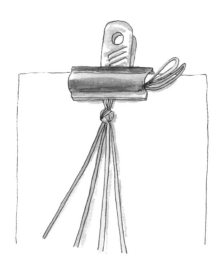

CLIPBOARD
Simply clip the top knot under the clip at the top and start braiding!

SAFETY PIN
This is our favorite way of working as you can braid on the sofa while listening to music or chatting with friends! Open your safety pin and hook all the ends of floss onto it, or thread the knot through if the ends are not doubled over. Then carefully pin the loop onto a pillow and close to secure.

CARD LOOM
Take a piece of card approximately 6 x 8 in (15 x 20 cm) and cut one notch in the center at the top edge. Then, evenly space out the number of notches you have threads for along the bottom. You may wish to make a loom with plenty of notches so you can use it for lots of different projects. Simply place the top knot in the central notch and put each string in one of the bottom notches. This is a good way of working if you are traveling as the threads do not get messed up and tangled and it gives you a surface to work on.

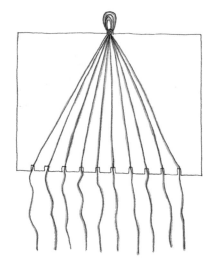

TAPE
Cut a piece of tape 5 cm (2 in) long and stick the thread ends onto the table. This will give you the tension you need to start braiding. Don't pull too hard or your threads will fall out!

techniques

17

HOW TO COMPLETE YOUR FRIENDSHIP BRACELETS

Once you have completed your braid you need to decide how to finish it and wear it! There are plenty of different methods.

LOOSE ENDS

This is the quickest and easiest way to finish your bracelet. Once you have finished braiding, simply tie a knot and trim the ends to 3 in (8 cm) long. They can then be threaded through the loop at the other end of the braid. Alternatively, before you start braiding, leave 3 in (8 cm) of thread. Finish your braid as before and tie the two sets of loose ends together.

BRAIDED ENDS: Method 1

Once you have finished braiding, tie a knot and then divide the threads into three equal-sized bundles. Braid (plait) the ends until you have a piece 3 in (8 cm) long and then tie another knot and trim. Thread this through the loop at the other end. You could also begin your bracelet with a 3-in (8-cm) long piece of three-way braid and then finish as before so that you can tie the two sets of braided ends together.

BRAIDED ENDS: Method 2

Once you have finished braiding, tie a knot and then divide the ends into six bundles and make two braids (plaits). Thread one through the loop at the start of the bracelet, then tie a knot or bow using the other braid to secure.

techniques

18

BUTTONS

1 Finish braiding, and then thread a button onto the floss.

2 Turn the braid over, tie a knot, and trim the thread ends.

2 Hook the loop at the start of the braid over the button to secure.

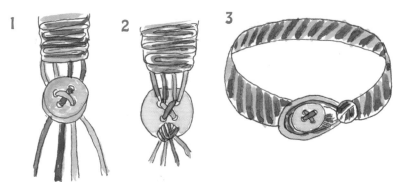

SLIDING KNOT

This is a great knot to use if the bracelet will be frequently put on and taken off.

1 Hold the cords next to each other and fold the one you want to make the knot over.

2 Loop the end around both cords.

3 Now loop it around twice more and thread the end through the original loop.

4 Pull tight until the knot is tight but can still move up and down the other cord.

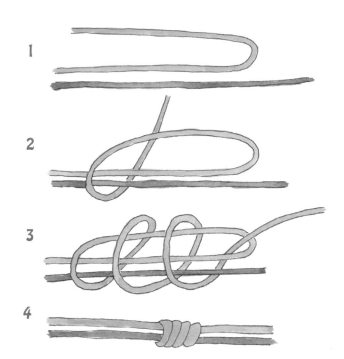

SNAP FASTENINGS

These are small round poppers that come in two parts. Stitch one half to one end of the braid and the other to the other end. Make sure you stitch them onto the opposite sides so that when the bracelet is wrapped round the wrist, the fastenings come together.

MACRAMÉ KNOT

Another adjustable knot is the macramé knot.

1 Overlap the two ends of the bracelet.

2 Take a second cord to make the knot and fold it in half, then make a lark's head knot (see page 11) over the ends of the bracelet.

3 Work three square knots (see page 13) over the cords.

4 Tie the cords in a tight knot and thread them back into the knot. Trim as short as possible.

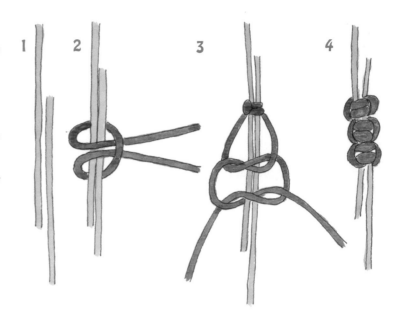

HOW TO DESIGN A BRAID

Here are some things to think about when you start designing your own braids.

1 Who is it for? We have included some projects more suited for boys if you want to make a gift for a brother or cousin, or your dad.

2 What is your skill level? Some braids are simpler to make than others. Try the easy ones to build your confidence then move onto the more difficult ones. Try using fewer colors and embellishments to begin with since this also makes them easier to achieve.

3 Before you begin your braid, gather all your materials together and check that you are happy with the colors, textures, and embellishments.

ALTERNATIVE USES FOR BRAIDS

Don't just stick to bracelets; try experimenting with the techniques shown in this book to make headbands, key chains, and more!

HEADBANDS
We have included a few headband braids in this book but if you want to make them from different types of braids, simply make your braid about 12 in (30 cm) long. Then stitch each end to a piece of elastic approximately 6 in (15 cm) long. Alternatively, to add a braid to a plastic headband, make a braid the same length as the headband and then glue or stitch it onto the band.

ANKLETS
Anklets are just slightly longer bracelets, make them 8 in (20 cm) long and tie around your ankle.

NECKLACES/CHOKERS
To work out the length of a necklace or choker, simply loosely wrap a thread around your neck, measure it, and add 8 in (20 cm) for tying.

BELTS
Create a Boho-style belt using some of the wider techniques and thicker materials explained in this book. Simply measure around your waist and add an extra 24 in (60 cm) for tying. You could also try adding a buckle to one end for an adjustable belt.

BAG STRAPS
Thicker braids are generally ideal for bag straps, but why not try threading a thinner braid through holes around a circular piece of fabric to make a jewelry pouch?

KEY CHAIN
Ideal for Father's Day, key chains are a really fun gift to make. Fold your braiding floss in half and, before tying a knot, thread on a metal split ring. Braid as normal for approximately 4 in (10 cm) and then tie and trim the ends.

WATCH STRAP
Broken watch strap? Make two braids approximately 3 in (8 cm) long and before knotting the ends, thread them through the slots on either side of the watch face. Sew the ends through the back of the back to secure them in place.

BOOKMARK
An ideal present for a bookworm or grown-up, wide flat braids make perfect bookmarks. You could try making the words bracelet shown on page 36 to personalize the bookmark with your chosen name. The bookmark should measure 6 in (15 cm) long.

GIFT-WRAP
Personalize your gift-wrapping by replacing the cord or ribbon round your gifts with a braid! The length will depend on the size of your parcel. A simple braid tied in a bow at the top would look so cute.

CHAPTER 1

so sweet

Spiral friendship braids • Chevron bracelets • Fishtail necklace and bracelet set • Braiding wheel bracelets • Fabric headband Woven words bracelets • V-macramé braids • Flower macramé braids Crochet and sequin bracelets • Braided jewelry bowl

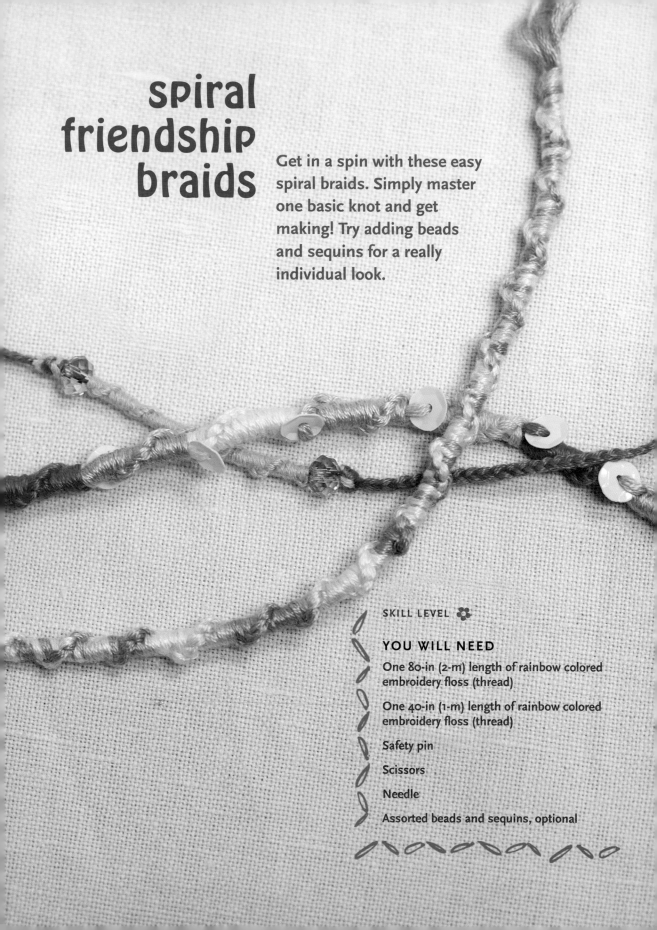

spiral friendship braids

Get in a spin with these easy spiral braids. Simply master one basic knot and get making! Try adding beads and sequins for a really individual look.

SKILL LEVEL

YOU WILL NEED

One 80-in (2-m) length of rainbow colored embroidery floss (thread)

One 40-in (1-m) length of rainbow colored embroidery floss (thread)

Safety pin

Scissors

Needle

Assorted beads and sequins, optional

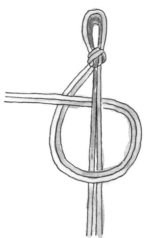

1 To make a plain spiral braid, fold the lengths of floss in half and tie in a knot at the top, leaving a hanging loop. The shorter lengths will form the base and the longer lengths will be the wrapping cords. Using a safety pin, attach the knot to a pillow.

2 Make a half-forward knot (see page 10) by looping the longer left-hand floss over and then under the right-hand floss. Poke the end through the loop formed on the left. Pull to tighten the knot.

3 Repeat step 2 until you have made the length of braid you want—approximately 6 in (15 cm). The braid will naturally twist as you repeat the knot, but this is the effect you want. Tie off the ends and trim with scissors for a tidy finish.

further ideas

* To add beads or sequins, simply slip them onto the wrapping threads and secure them in place by tying a figure of four knot.

* To use the spiral as a feature, cut four pieces of floss—three red and one blue. Tie the three red pieces of floss in a knot and braid them for 2 in (5 cm). Then tie in a blue piece of floss with a knot. Thread on a bead and start spiraling (see steps 2–3) for 2 in (5 cm). Thread on another bead, tie a knot, and continue braiding the red floss for another 2 in (5 cm). Secure with a final knot and trim the blue floss as short as possible.

* Create a striped braid by cutting and tying a number of different colored floss together. Then knot as before, using one of the colors to knot and the others to create the base thread to knot around. Change the knotting floss as often as you wish to vary the stripe.

This is one of the most basic techniques of braiding—the double knot—but once you start you just won't be able to stop making these chevron braids! Try mixing up the colors, adding beads, or just keep it simple.

chevron bracelets

SKILL LEVEL ❀❀

YOU WILL NEED

One 40-in (1-m) length of embroidery floss (thread) in each of the following colors: lilac, yellow, pink, turquoise, peach, and lime green

Safety pin

Scissors

Assorted beads and rhinestone chain, optional

1 Fold the floss in half and tie in a knot at the top. Using the safety pin, attach the knot to a pillow. Arrange the floss so that the lilac threads are on the outside, followed by one strand of each color in the same order from the outside to the center on each side.

2 Make a forward knot (see page 10). Starting with the left-hand floss (lilac), loop it around the second floss in the sequence. Pull the loop tightly to the top of the second floss.

3 Make a second loop in the lilac floss so you have made two knots.

Embellish your finished bracelets with rhinestone chains, sequins, and beads for a more glamorous look!

4 Repeat steps 2 and 3 in turn on the third, fourth, fifth, and sixth lengths of floss on the left-hand side, knotting left to right. Stop when you have knotted across all of the left-hand threads—the left-hand lilac floss should now be in the center.

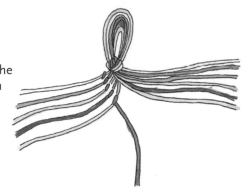

5 Now repeat steps 2 and 3 again, but work in reverse, using a backward knot (see page 10), so the right-hand lilac floss is looped twice in the opposite way around the second floss in the sequence. Work your way into the center, stopping when you reach the center of the braid.

6 Make two loops with the left-hand lilac thread over the right-hand lilac thread to close the chevron. Continue working rows like this until your braid is long enough to go around your wrist (approximately 3–4 in/ 8–10 cm). Divide the remaining threads into three and braid (plait) for 2 in (5 cm). Tie a knot and trim the excess.

7 Stitch a piece of rhinestone chain along the center of the bracelet using matching floss.

further ideas

* Create a mismatched chevron by mixing up the colors so they don't match up on either side. For example, on one side you could have red, green, yellow, and blue and on the other green, blue, red, and yellow.

* Add beads to the braid by threading them onto the outer floss before looping it through to the center.

* Create thicker stripes by having two or three lengths of floss of the same color next to each other (see the bracelet on the left on the previous page).

This necklace and bracelet set would be a fantastic gift for a friend. Add a modern twist to a traditional fishtail braid by adding a metal chain as one of your threads.

fishtail necklace and bracelet set

SKILL LEVEL ✿✿

YOU WILL NEED

For the necklace

Six 30-in (75-cm) lengths of embroidery floss (thread) in each of the following colors: pale pink, mint green, jade green, coral, and yellow

Two 30-in (75-cm) pieces of gold curb chain

17³⁄₄ in (45 cm) yellow ribbon

Safety pin

Scissors

For the bracelet

Two 40-in (1-m) lengths of embroidery floss (thread) in each of the following colors: pale pink, mint green, jade green, coral, and yellow

Safety pin

Scissors

NECKLACE INSTRUCTIONS

1 Tie the lengths of floss together with a loose knot in the top, leaving a 4-in (10-cm) tail. Using the safety pin, attach the knot to a pillow. Then arrange the floss into two bundles so you have three of each color in each bundle.

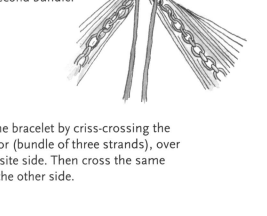

2 Thread the chain onto one of the bundles of floss, and repeat with the other chain on the second bundle.

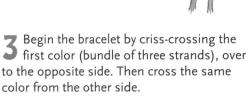

3 Begin the bracelet by criss-crossing the first color (bundle of three strands), over to the opposite side. Then cross the same color from the other side.

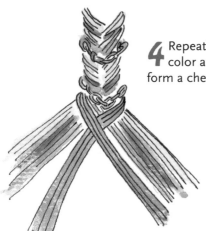

4 Repeat step 3 with each color and the chains to form a chevron pattern.

5 Once you have enough braid for the necklace—approximately 12 in (30 cm)—thread a bundle of floss through the last chain link as you did at the start. Trim off any excess.

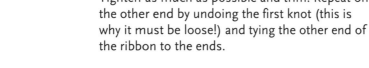

6 Trim the ends to 4 in (10 cm) and then tie one end of the ribbon to the threads with a knot. Tighten as much as possible and trim. Repeat on the other end by undoing the first knot (this is why it must be loose!) and tying the other end of the ribbon to the ends.

BRACELET INSTRUCTIONS

1 Fold the floss in half and tie a knot at the top. Using the safety pin, attach the knot to a pillow. Then arrange the floss into two bundles so you have two of each color in each bundle.

2 Begin the bracelet by criss-crossing the first color (bundle of two strands), over to the opposite side. Then cross the same color from the other side. Repeat with each color to create a chevron pattern.

3 Once you have enough braid to wrap around your wrist, approximately 6 in (15 cm), tie a knot in the end and trim the excess floss. Knot the ends together to form a bracelet.

"Kumihimo" is the Japanese name for these cords, made on a braiding wheel, and they were traditionally used by Samurai warriors to lace their armor and kimonos. Give them a more modern look by using brightly colored floss.

braiding wheel bracelets

SKILL LEVEL ✿

YOU WILL NEED

Templates (page 124)

Corrugated card

PVA glue or double-sided tape

Scissors

Sixteen 20-in (50-cm) lengths of embroidery floss (thread) in various colors (check your braiding wheel to see how many of each color you need)

1 To make the braiding wheels, photocopy the templates on page 124. Stick each one to the corrugated card with glue or double-sided tape. Once dry, if using glue, cut them out.

2 Select a braiding wheel and count how many notches of each color there are in order to work out how many lengths of embroidery floss for each color you will need. For example, the heart design has ten peach notches and six pink notches, so you'll need ten lengths of peach floss and six lengths of pink floss. Cut each floss 20 in (50 cm) long and tie in a knot 2 in (5 cm) from the end.

3 Place the knot in the center of the wheel, then pull each length of floss and hook it in the color-corresponding petal. Each petal has two notches and each floss should have its own notch.

A   B

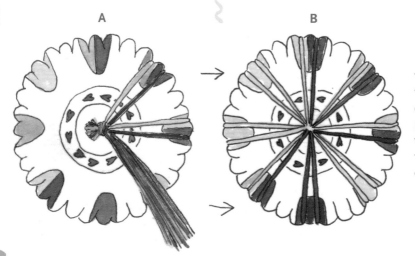

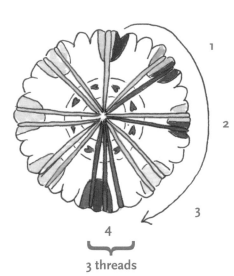

4 Unhook a length of floss from a right petal and rehook it on the right of the floss on the opposite petal (the beginning of the fourth set of threads). This creates a group of three strands.

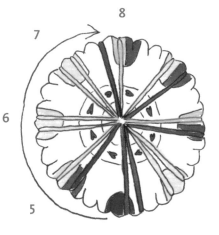

5 Unhook the floss on the left of the bottom group and hook it in the notch to the left of the single floss.

Need a rest? Stop when there are three threads on the bottom notch. When you come back to braiding, you will know where to start from (see step 5).

6 Rotate the wheel counter-clockwise by one petal and repeat steps 4 and 5. You will see that gradually the pattern appears.

7 Braid until your bracelet is long enough to wrap around your wrist loosely, usually 6 in (15 cm). Then tie the ends in a knot and trim to 3 in (8 cm). Knot the ends together to form a bracelet.

8 Try out the different braiding wheels—the principle is the same but the arrangement of floss colors at the start changes the pattern created.

fabric headband

Turn heads with this vintage-look braided headband! Made from strips of scrap fabric, this headband is so easy to make and has a pretty sparkle.

SKILL LEVEL 🌸

YOU WILL NEED

Three 36 x 2-in (80 x 5-cm) pieces of patterned cotton fabric

Safety pin

Scissors

Needle

Sewing thread

6 in (15 cm) elastic

All-purpose glue, optional

Assorted sequins and beads

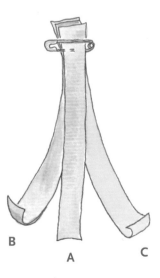

1 Layer the pieces of fabric together and attach to a pillow with the safety pin.

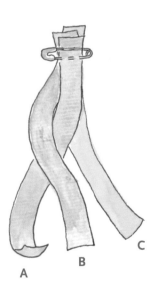

2 Start with the left-hand thread (B) and bring it into the center.

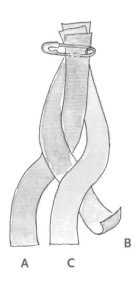

3 Then move the right-hand thread (C) into the center.

4 Repeat steps 2 and 3 until you have a braid approximately 12 in (30 cm) long. Trim the ends, fold over each other, and sew securely in place on the underside of the braid. Repeat with the other ends attached to your pillow.

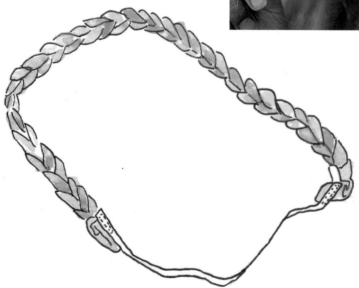

5 Sew the elastic to the ends of the braid. You may have to shorten your elastic according to the size of your head. Embellish your braided headband by sewing or sticking on sequins and beads.

fabric headband

35

woven words bracelets

Personalize your braids using this method of adding words. A combination of backward and forward knots, these are easier to make than you think!

SKILL LEVEL ✿✿

YOU WILL NEED

Templates (page 125)

One 26-ft (8-m) length of embroidery floss (thread) in blue (the background color)

Five 58-in (1.2-m) lengths of embroidery floss (thread) in lilac

Posterboard (card) loom, measuring 6 x 8 in (15 x 20 cm) —1 notch at the top and 10 at the bottom (see page 15 for how to make a loom)

Scissors

1 Create your pattern by copying the letter templates shown on page 125. It is best to leave one or two rows of background color between each letter and four rows between each word.

2 Fold the lilac floss in half and tie in a knot at the top. Hook the knot into the top notch on your card loom and fan out the others so they each have their own notch.

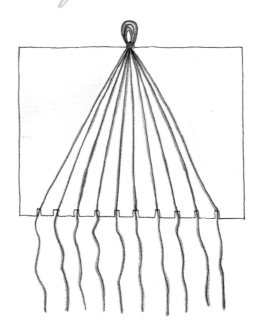

so sweet

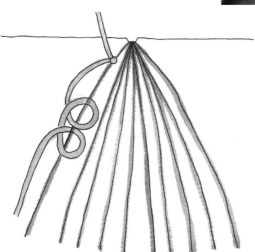

3 Tie the background color to the top left-hand floss and work a row of forward knots (left, see page 10). Then work a row of backward knots (right, see page 10). Repeat until you have five rows of blue floss.

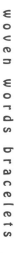

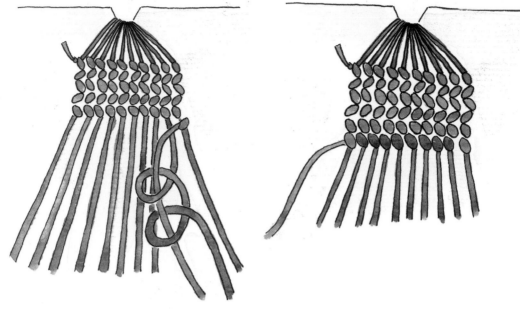

4 To make the first row of your first letter, work one backward knot (this makes a blue stitch) on the first lilac thread of the row. Then unhook the second lilac floss and work a forward knot with it to create a lilac stitch. Then put the thread back in its notch. Unhook the third lilac floss and work another forward knot and place it back in its notch and so on, following your pattern. For example, for the first row of a "B," you should make one blue backward knot, eight lilac forward knots, and one blue backward knot.

5 Keep following the pattern. So to continue a "B," for example, on the next row, work forward knots with the blue and backward knots with the lilac floss; the pattern will be one blue, one lilac, three blue, one lilac, two blue, one lilac, one blue.

6 Continue working these alternate rows while following your pattern until the lettering is complete.

7 Once your word is complete, weave another 10 or more rows using the blue floss only. Knot to secure and trim the end of the blue floss tidily. Then, divide the lilac floss into two bunches and braid (plait) each one for 3 in (8 cm). Knot and trim the floss to complete.

further ideas

* Try "writing" your name or a friend's name into a bracelet.

A simple but effective technique that creates V-shaped knots. Try adding beads and charms to make your bracelets really special.

v-macramé braids

SKILL LEVEL ✿

YOU WILL NEED

One 30-in (75-cm) length of embroidery floss in each of the following colors: green, orange, fluorescent pink, and fluorescent yellow

Two 16-in (40-cm) lengths of embroidery floss in yellow

Safety pin

Scissors

1 Tie the floss together in a knot 3 in (8 cm) from the end. Attach the loop to a pillow using the safety pin.

2 Group the floss so the short yellow floss is in the center; to the left is the pink and orange floss and to the right is the green and yellow floss.

3 Take the left-hand pink and orange floss and make a forward knot (see page 10).

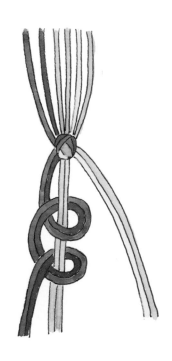

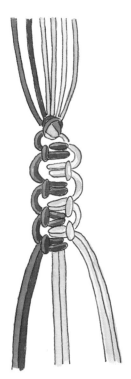

further ideas

* To add beads, slide wide-holed beads along the bracelet once you have finished braiding (see step 5) but before you tie a knot in the end. Space out the beads and tie a knot to secure, leaving a shorter end than on the main project.

 **4** Then take the right-hand green and yellow floss and make a backward knot (see page 10).

5 Repeat steps 3 and 4 to make a V-shaped pattern. Keep braiding until your bracelet measures approximately 6 in (15 cm) long. Tie a knot in the end and trim, leaving 3-in (8-cm) ends for tying.

v-macramé braids

41

flower macramé braids

These macramé braids are dotted with little flowers and look so pretty and delicate.

SKILL LEVEL ❀❀

YOU WILL NEED

One 60-in (1.5-m) length of embroidery floss (thread) in each of the following colors: coral, yellow, and green

Safety pin

Scissors

1 Fold your floss in half and attach the loop to a pillow with the safety pin.

2 Arrange your floss into the following order—green, coral, yellow, yellow, coral, and green.

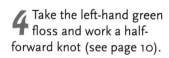

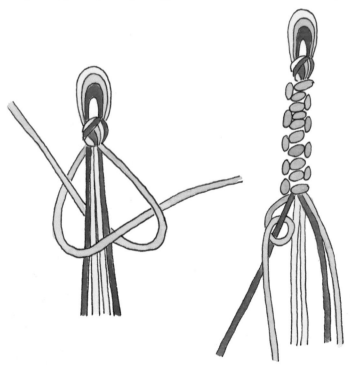

3 Work ten square knots (see page 13) with the outer green floss.

4 Take the left-hand green floss and work a half-forward knot (see page 10).

5 Take the right-hand green floss and work a half-backward knot (see page 10). The order of the threads is now coral, green, yellow, yellow, green, coral.

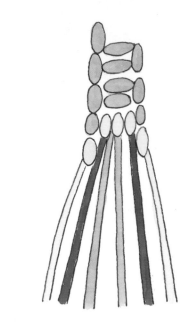
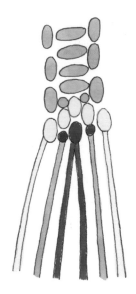
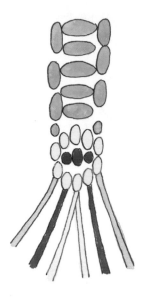

5 Work a forward knot with the two central yellow threads, then work two backward knots with the left-hand yellow floss, and then two forward knots with the right-hand yellow floss.

6 Work a half-forward knot with the left-hand coral floss and a half-backward knot with the right-hand coral floss so they are in the center of the braid. Forward knot them together.

7 Work two forward knots with the left-hand yellow floss and two backward knots with the right-hand yellow floss. Forward knot them together to complete your first flower.

8 Work ten square knots with the green floss.

9 Rearrange the floss for the next flower to green, yellow, coral, coral, yellow, green, and make a yellow flower by repeating steps 4–7.

10 Continue with this pattern until your bracelet is approximately 6 in (15 cm) long. Tie in a knot to complete and trim the ends.

crochet and sequin bracelets

Using a simple crochet chain stitch and a few sequins, you can create this stunning bracelet! Make it long enough to wrap round your wrist two or three times to create a layered look.

SKILL LEVEL ✿✿

YOU WILL NEED

One 80-in (2-m) length of embroidery floss (thread) in a natural color

100 assorted colored sequins in pink, peach, blue, and green

C/2 (3mm) crochet hook

Needle

Scissors

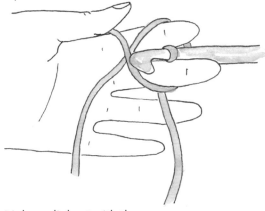

1 Make a slipknot with the floss and insert the crochet hook (see page 14).

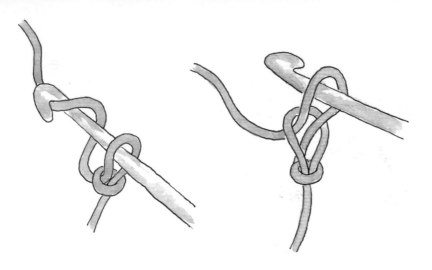

2 Make a chain of 15 stitches. This is done by wrapping the floss over the hook and pulling it through the loop on the hook.

3 Thread the needle with the other end of the floss and thread the sequins onto it.

4 Continue crocheting a chain but each time you make a stitch, push a sequin up and secure it in place with the stitch.

5 Continue with this process until your bracelet is long enough to wrap around your wrist two or three times, approximately 20 in (50 cm). Pull the floss through the last stitch to secure.

further ideas

* Add beads to the crochet chain instead of sequins for a slightly chunkier bracelet.

* Use sequins or beads only in a color that matches the floss for a more understated look.

so sweet

Store all your new braids and bracelets in this pretty braided bowl—it is made entirely from forward and backward knots!

braided jewelry bowl

SKILL LEVEL ✿✿✿

YOU WILL NEED

Fourteen 60-in (1.5-m) lengths of cotton knitting yarn in each of the following colors: cream, lime green, mint green, turquoise, lilac, pink, and yellow

Needle

Scissors

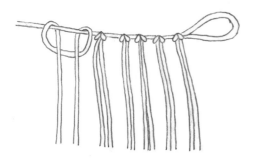

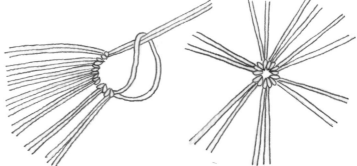

1 Fold one of the cream lengths of yarn in half. Knot the other six cream threads onto it using a lark's head knot (see page 11).

2 Thread the ends of the first cream yarn through the loop at the other end and pull to tighten.

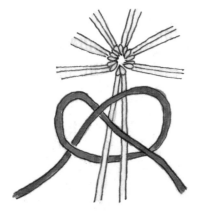

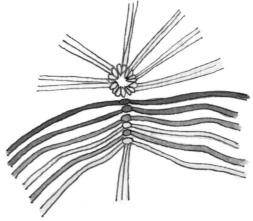

3 Tie one of each colored yarn onto one set of cream threads using a simple reef knot, as shown.

so sweet

48

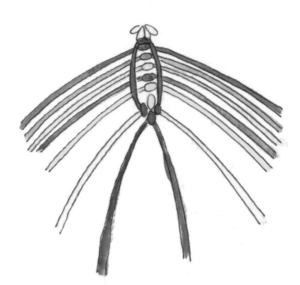

4 Work a backward knot (see page 10) with the two cream threads.

5 Start to create a chevron using the pink yarn: work one forward knot (see page 10) for the left of the "V" and one backward knot for the right of the "V". Join the pink yarn with a backward knot.

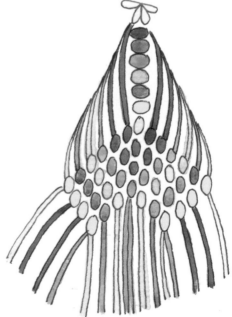

6 Continue the chevron by working two forward knots and two backward knots with the lilac yarn. Join with a backward knot. Then work three forward knots and three backward knots with the blue yarn. Join with a backward knot.

7 Make only four forward and backward knots on each side of the "V" with the mint green, lime green, and yellow yarn. Repeat steps 2–4 on each of the other six "petals" of the bowl.

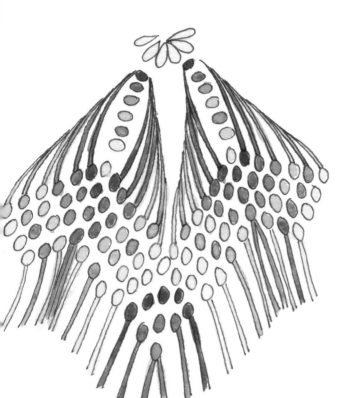

8 Now join the petals together by taking the cream yarn, tying a backward knot, and then making a reverse chevron with them. To do this, make three backward knots on the left-hand threads and three forward knots on the right-hand threads. Repeat with the pink yarn but make only two knots on each side. Using the lilac yarn, make one knot on each side, and then finally backward knot the blue threads together.

9 Repeat step 8 in reverse. Using the lilac yarn, work one forward knot on the left and one backward knot on the right. Join with a backward knot. Using the pink yarn, work two forward knots on the left and two backward knots on the right. Join with a backward knot. Repeat this knotting process, increasing the number of knots by one each time using the cream, yellow, lime green, mint green, and blue yarn.

10 Repeat step 9 to make the other petals around the central flower.

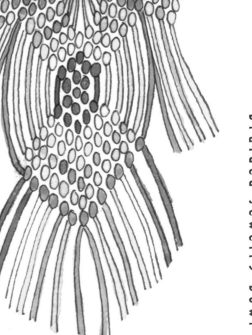

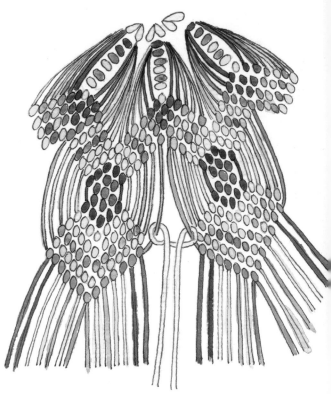

11 Now, take another length of cream yarn and tie it onto the blue yarn between the petals to create a base cord.

12 Tie a yellow, lime green, mint green, blue, lilac, and pink yarn onto the cream thread as in step 2. Work a backward knot with the two cream threads as in step 4.

13 Create a reverse chevron with the threads. To do this, start with the yellow yarn and make one backward knot with the left-hand yarn and one forward knot with the right-hand yarn. Join with a backward knot. Repeat with the remaining threads, increasing the number of knots by one on each row.

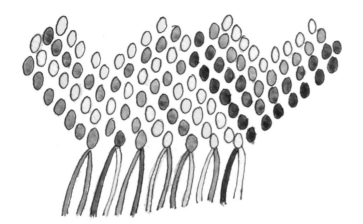

14 Repeat steps 12–13 for the other petals.

15 To fill in the "V" shapes on the bowl, take the yarn in the corner of the "V" and make backward knots on the next six threads. Then take the second yarn on the left of the "V" and work five backward knots, then 5, 4, 3, 2, and 1. Repeat on each "V" until you have made a flat edge.

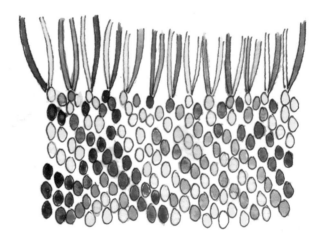

16 Now work alternate rows of forward knots and backward knots all around the edge of the bowl until the sides are the height you want. The bowl pictured here has ten rows of forward knots and ten rows of backward knots.

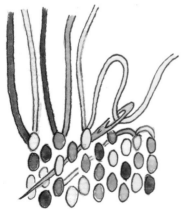

17 To complete your bowl, sew the ends of the yarn through the stitches with a needle, and trim.

CHAPTER 2

tribal attitude

Dream catcher bracelets • Beaded leather cuff

String square knot braids • Woven stud bracelet • Brass nut

bracelets • Boho headband • Peruvian braid barefoot sandals

Leaf bracelets • Josephine braids

dream catcher bracelets

Keep your dreams sweet by wearing one of these dazzling dream catcher braids! Try making larger or smaller ones by using different-sized rings. It would look great as a choker or belt, too!

SKILL LEVEL ✿✿

YOU WILL NEED

Split rings or metal rings, 2¼ in (3 cm) in diameter

Embroidery floss (thread) in various colors—brown, orange, cream, turquoise—and thicknesses

Assorted beads

Scissors

Needle

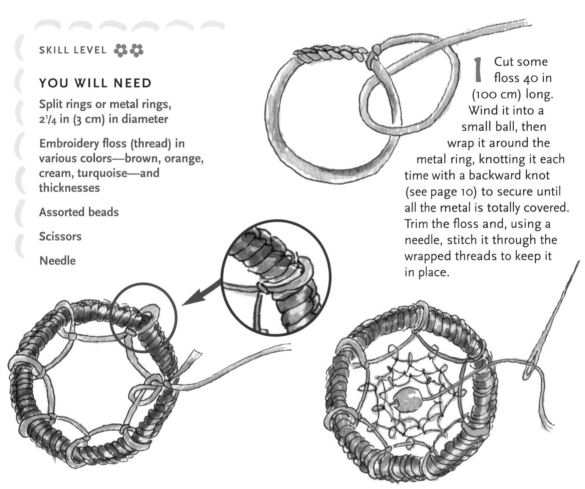

1 Cut some floss 40 in (100 cm) long. Wind it into a small ball, then wrap it around the metal ring, knotting it each time with a backward knot (see page 10) to secure until all the metal is totally covered. Trim the floss and, using a needle, stitch it through the wrapped threads to keep it in place.

2 Select your floss for the "web" and tie the end to the ring. Thread the other end onto a needle and wind it around the ring approximately seven times, looping it to secure. Tie the end of the floss to the floss at the beginning of the ring where you started.

3 Repeat this looping of the floss on the next row but wrap it around the first row of loops rather than the metal ring. Continue until the ring is filled. Using the needle, thread on a bead and secure it in the center of the dream catcher before tying off.

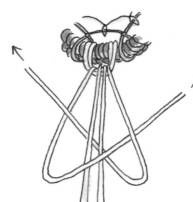

5 Tie a square knot (see page 13). Take the long left-hand length of floss and make a figure of four over the shorter base threads. Then carry the other floss under the two base cords and through the center of the figure of four. Pull both lengths of floss tight to secure.

4 To make the strap, cut a piece of floss 15 in (38 cm) long and another piece 41½ in (105 cm) long. Fold them in half together and loop them through the metal ring as shown, using a lark's head knot (see page 11).

6 Repeat in the reverse using the long right-hand thread. Make a reverse figure of four with the right-hand floss and then take the left-hand length and put it underneath the base cords and pull tight to secure.

7 Continue with these two knots until your bracelet measures approximately 3 in (8 cm). Tie the floss in a knot to secure and trim the excess. Repeat with the other two lengths of floss on the other side of the dream catcher to complete your bracelet.

further ideas

* Try using different-sized rings for more delicate or chunkier bracelets.

* Try braiding (plaiting) or a spiral twist knot for the strap to vary the look and skill.

* Make a longer cord strap and use the dream catcher as a choker or belt.

This leather cuff will add a cool and trendy edge to a summer outfit. Create the beaded section using a bead loom—these can be easily picked up at your local craft store—then stitch the beaded band to a piece of leather.

beaded leather cuff

1 Cut eight lengths of sewing thread 18 in (45 cm) long and tie together in a knot. Divide the bunch in two and hook the knot over the end nail on the roller of the bead loom. Then slot each thread into a groove of the loom.

SKILL LEVEL ✿✿

YOU WILL NEED

Bead loom (see page 15)

Strong sewing thread

Needle

Glass seed beads in blue, red, orange, white green, turquoise, and yellow

8 x 1¼-in (20 x 4-cm) piece of leather

Scissors

Two snap fasteners (press studs)

2 Wind the roller until you have about 6 in (15 cm) of thread remaining. Pull the threads tight and tie a knot in the other end. Hook the knot over the nail on the other roller. Place each thread into a groove on that end of the loom, ensuring they are straight and not twisted, and then tighten the roller until all the threads are taut.

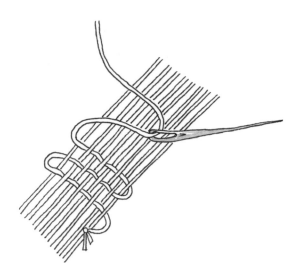

3 Cut another length of sewing thread 18 in (45 cm) long and tie it onto the outer thread on the loom. With the help of a needle, weave through the warp threads (threads going vertically in the weaving) two to three times to create a base.

4 Thread on your beads for the first row, and then place them underneath the warp threads, making sure that each bead is between two threads.

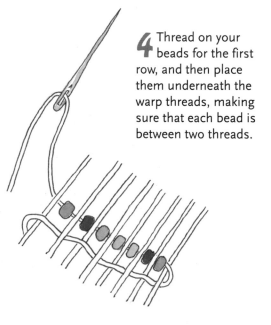

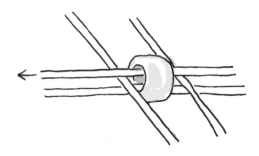

5 Take the needle back through the beads but over the top of the warp threads to secure them in position.

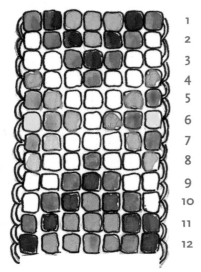

1
2
3
4
5
6
7
8
9
10
11
12

6 Follow the beading sequence, shown above, three times to create a piece of beading 36 rows long (approximately 4 in/10 cm). Weave a few extra rows of thread as you did at the start, and then tie the thread onto the outer warp thread and trim.

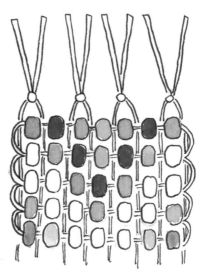

7 Cut the beading from the loom and knot the ends together.

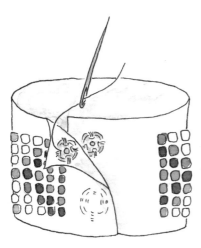

8 Sew the beading to the center of the leather strip. Complete by sewing on two snap fasteners (press studs) to the inside ends of the cuff.

string square knot braids

These chunky string braids are ideal for girls and boys. Here, we have added beads and buttons to add texture and color, but the braids look just as good on their own.

SKILL LEVEL ✿

YOU WILL NEED

24-in (60-cm) piece of string

36-in (80-cm) piece of string

Safety pin

Assorted beads and buttons

Scissors

Needle

1 Fold the pieces of string in half together and tie them in a knot to secure. Attach the knot to a pillow with the safety pin.

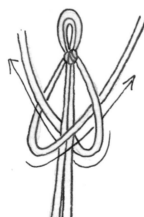

2 Make a square knot (see page 13). Take the long left-hand string and make a figure of four over the shorter base strings. Then carry the other string under the two base pieces and through the center of the figure of four. Pull both pieces of string tight to secure.

3 Repeat this process in the reverse using the long right-hand piece of string. Make a reverse figure of four with the right-hand string and then take the left one and put it underneath the base string. Pull tight to secure.

4 Thread a few beads or buttons onto the base strings and knot them in place as you braid.

tribal attitude

further ideas

5 Continue with these two knots until your braid measures approximately 6 in (15 cm). Tie the string in a knot to secure. Trim to 1 in (2.5 cm). Push the knot through the loop to secure around your wrist.

* Repeat step 2 only to create a twisted braid rather than a square one. Include beads, if you wish, threaded onto the base string as you work.

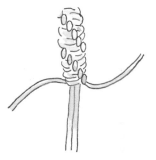

woven stud bracelet

Learn the ancient craft of weaving and create your own woven braid. Decorate with metal studs to finish. Why not try making a longer braid to use as a belt? It would also make a great guitar strap for music lovers.

SKILL LEVEL ✿✿

YOU WILL NEED

Loom made from a piece of card 8 x 3 in (20 x 8 cm) with 14 notches cut into each short end approximately ⅛-in (2-mm) apart (see page 15)

10-count cotton crochet thread in yellow, green, burgundy, turquoise, and gray

Yarn needle

Metal pyramid studs in assorted sizes

1 Wrap the yellow crochet thread around the card loom, making sure that there is one thread in each notch. Then tie a knot diagonally in the center to secure. These threads are referred to as the warp.

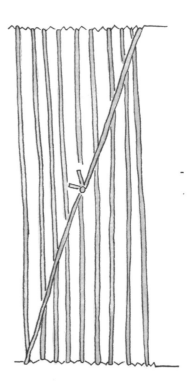

tribal attitude

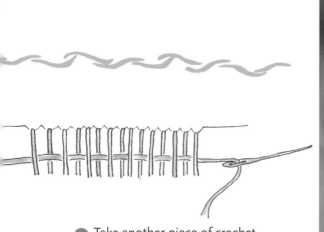

2 Take another piece of crochet thread, approximately 20 in (50 cm) long, and thread the needle. Weave the crochet thread under and over the warp threads. These threads are called the weft.

3 Take the needle and thread it over and under the next rows working in the opposite direction to the row above. This secures the weft in place. Keep repeating these two rows.

4 Change the color of the crochet thread as often as you wish. Here, we've made some bands of color thicker and others narrower, but you may prefer a more even look.

5 Once your weaving is long enough to wrap around your wrist, approximately 6 in (15 cm), cut the warp threads off the loom in the center of the back so they are long. Knot each pair of threads together to keep the weaving tight and in place. Then trim the ends to 3 in (8 cm).

6 Arrange the pyramid studs along the length of the braid. Press down through to the back, and then fold the points inward to fix in place.

woven stud bracelet

brass nut bracelets

Add an edgy look to your braids with these brass nut bracelets. Simply add them in bunches as you work for a more delicate result.

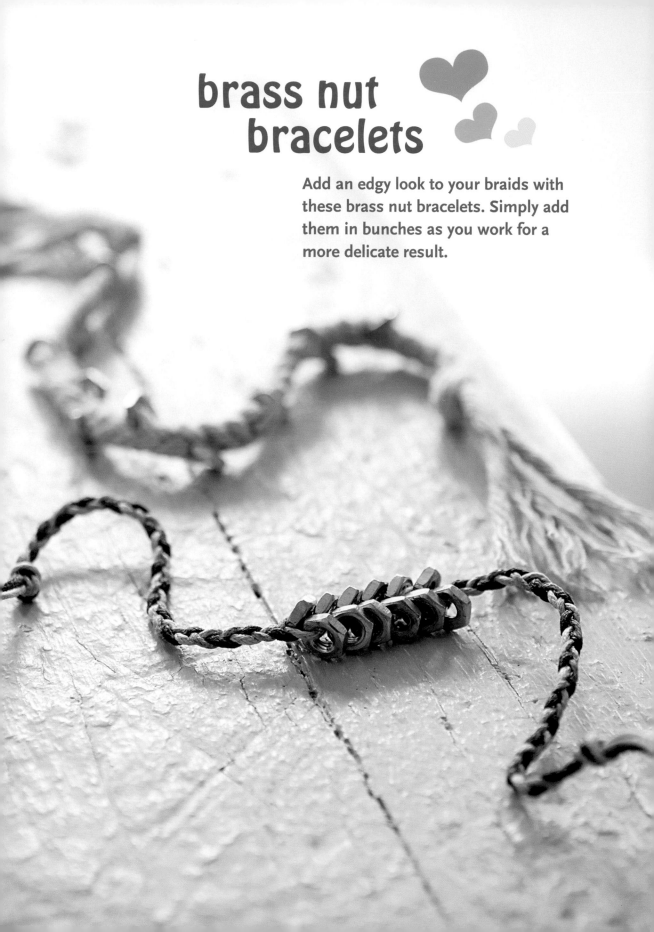

SKILL LEVEL ❀❀

YOU WILL NEED

One 20-in (50-cm) length
of waxed cord in each
of the following colors:
beige, turquoise,
and khaki

Safety pin

Scissors

Twelve brass nuts (M4
or ¹⁄₄-in/4-mm size)

1 Tie the three cords
together in a knot at the
top. Using a safety pin,
attach the knot to a pillow.

B   A   C   B   C   A

2 Braid (plait) the cords together. Start
with the blue cord (A) and move it into
the center, over the beige cord (B). Then
move the khaki cord (C) into the center, over
the blue cord. Keep repeating this process,
moving the left-hand cord into the center and
then the right-hand cord into the center, until
your braid is approximately 3 in (8 cm) long.

3 Thread six nuts onto each cord and
continue braiding, but each time you
bring a cord into the center, pull a nut up
and secure it into the braid. Repeat until
you have secured all of the nuts in place.
Then braid the remaining cords for
another 3 in (8 cm), or until finished.
Tie the cords in a knot to secure.

further ideas

* Rather than positioning all of the brass nuts together,
spread them along your braid.

* Try using different cords, threads, and yarns, such as string
or embroidery floss, for a chunkier or more delicate-looking
bracelet. You could experiment with different-sized nuts, too.

brass nut bracelets

Get ready for the summer with this funky Boho-inspired headband. This four thread braided technique is slightly more time consuming than normal braids, but creates a wider headband that looks great with the added beads, bells, and feathers.

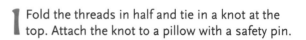

SKILL LEVEL ✿✿✿

YOU WILL NEED

One 60-in (1.5-m) length of yarn in each of the following colors: orange, cream, yellow, and brown

Safety pin

Assorted beads

Small bells

Feathers

Scissors

All-purpose glue, optional

boho headband

1 Fold the threads in half and tie in a knot at the top. Attach the knot to a pillow with a safety pin.

2 Label each pair of strands as A (orange), B (cream), C (yellow), and D (brown). Thread a variety of beads and bells onto each pair to pull up into the braid when required.

C   A D B

CDB   A

D B A C

3 Begin by taking strand C and placing it over strand B and then under strand A. B is then taken over strand D.

4 Take A and weave it under D and over B.

5 Take C and weave it over D, under B, and over A.

6 Repeat the move with D, weaving it over B, under A, and over C. Push a bell or bead up into the braiding at this point and weave it into position.

7 Continue weaving the left-hand strand of the braid over, under, and over, repeating step 6 every three or four weaves, until your braid measures approximately 40 in (1 m) in length. Tie in a knot and trim the ends.

8 Poke the feathers into the ends of the braid—they should stay in position but you may wish to glue them, too.

9 Wrap the finished braid around your head and tie it in a knot to secure.

peruvian braid barefoot sandals ♥

Braids aren't just for your wrists; create these beautiful macramé barefoot sandals that look great on the beach or at a picnic.

SKILL LEVEL ✿✿✿

YOU WILL NEED

Two 78-in (2-m) lengths of embroidery floss (thread) in each of these colors: lime, orange, purple, blue, cream, and brown

Four 12-in (30-cm) pieces of waxed cord/string (any color as it will not be seen)

Safety pin

Scissors

Needle

Matching sewing thread

2 x large star charms

1 Arrange your floss so you have two bunches of six threads, one of each color. Braid (plait) the central 4 in (10 cm), then fold it in half and tie the ends together where they meet. Add two of the cord/string pieces to this knot. This creates your toe loop. Divide the threads into two bunches with one of each color.

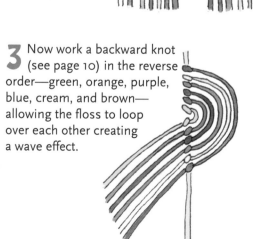

A B

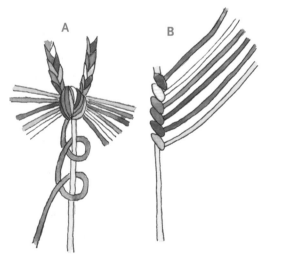

2 Secure the threads to a pillow with the safety pin. Start with the left-hand bunch and work a forward knot (see page 10) over the central waxed cord using the brown floss (A). Repeat with the cream, blue, purple, orange, and green threads (B).

3 Now work a backward knot (see page 10) in the reverse order—green, orange, purple, blue, cream, and brown—allowing the floss to loop over each other creating a wave effect.

4 Repeat steps 2 and 3 until your braid measures 5 in (12 cm). Tie a knot and trim the waxed cord as short as possible. Braid the remaining threads until they are long enough to wrap around your ankle and tie in a bow (approximately 20 in/50 cm long), then tie a knot and trim the ends. Repeat with the seven threads on the other side.

5 Sew the star charm onto the knot near the toe piece to complete. Repeat to make the second sandal with the second bunch of threads.

leaf bracelets

You'll "fall" in love with these leaf bracelets, which use backward and forward knots to create a cool braid.

SKILL LEVEL ✿✿

YOU WILL NEED

One 80-in (2-m) length of embroidery floss (thread) in each of the following colors: burgundy, red, orange, yellow, and white

Safety pin

Scissors

1 Fold your floss in half and tie a knot in the top. Attach it to a pillow using the safety pin.

2 Arrange your threads into the following order—burgundy, red, orange, yellow, white, white, yellow, orange, red, and burgundy.

3 Work a forward knot (see page 10) with the two central white threads.

4 Then work a forward knot with the left-hand yellow floss and a backward knot (see page 10) with the right-hand yellow floss. Join them in the center with a forward knot.

tribal attitude

72

5 Work two forward knots with the left-hand orange floss and two backward knots with the right-hand orange floss. Join them in the center with a forward knot.

6 Continue with the forward and backward knots, increasing by one knot each time until the burgundy threads are in the center.

7 Repeat steps 3–6 but in reverse color order, so the next leaf is red, orange, yellow, and white.

8 Repeat the braiding process until your bracelet is the desired length, approximately 6 in (15 cm). Tie in a knot and trim the ends.

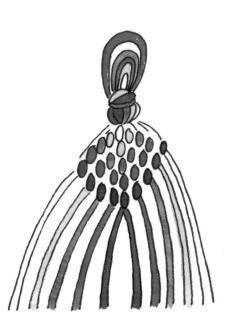

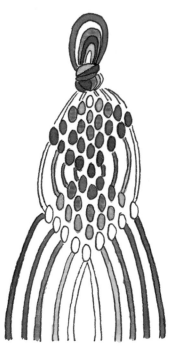

These knotted braids are ideal for girls or boys and can be made with one folded thread, or with six cords for a chunkier bracelet.

josephine braids

SKILL LEVEL ✿✿

YOU WILL NEED

One 40-in (1-m) length of waxed cord or string

Safety pin

Scissors

1 Fold your cord in half and tie a knot in the top. Attach the knot to a pillow using the safety pin. It is easier to work this knot sideways rather than vertically.

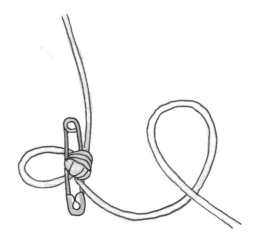

2 Take the left-hand, or lower, cord and create a loop.

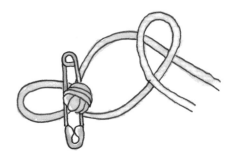

3 Then take the second cord underneath the loop.

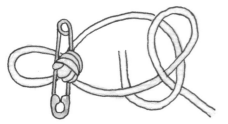

4 Wrap it over and then under the tails of the first loop.

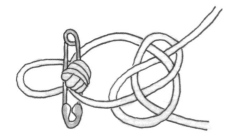

5 Finally, wrap it over and under to complete your first knot.

6 Repeat steps 2–5 until your bracelet measures 6 in (15 cm). Tie a knot to secure, and trim the cords to 3 in (8 cm).

CHAPTER 3

nautical knots

Wrapped braids • Nautical knot headband

Diagonal striped braids • Cross-stitched chains

Alternating square knot braid • Loop charm bracelets

Bar links bracelet • Twisted cord anchor bracelet

wrapped braids

YOU WILL NEED

One 16-in (40-cm) length of leather thong

Embroidery floss (thread) in red, white, and blue

Scissors

Needle

Assorted beads, optional

Boys can braid, too. These chunky wrapped cord wristbands look great with casual clothes, and are so easy to make. The leather thong gives the band a tough look—no girly braids here!

1 Fold one half of the leather thong back on itself to the center point, and then thread the other end through the loop and pull to the center point to meet the other end. This forms the base for your braid.

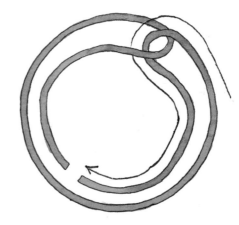

2 Knot a length of blue floss onto the braid base as shown.

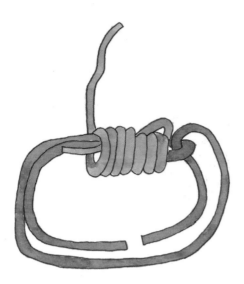

3 Wrap the floss round the base tightly, covering up the loose thread end until you want to change to the next color.

4 Keep repeating the knot-and-wrapping sequence until you have completed the wristband. Using a needle, thread the end of the floss back under the wrapped floss to secure. Trim the end with scissors.

further ideas

* Make the base braid in unbleached string, and then decorate it with a few rows of running stitch in blue and red embroidery floss.

* Add beads to the braid—thread them onto the leather thong before interlocking the ends, and then incorporate them into the design by wrapping the floss between them.

nautical knot headband

The nautical look is always on trend, and so will you be with this cute nautical knot headband. Simply follow the step-by-step instructions to create this fabulous and fashionable accessory.

SKILL LEVEL ✿✿

YOU WILL NEED

Two 25-in (65-cm) lengths of ¼-in (6-mm) twisted cord in each of the following colors: cream, blue, and red

6 in (15 cm) white elastic

Scissors

Sewing machine or needle

Strong sewing thread

Two 2-in (5-cm) squares of cream felt

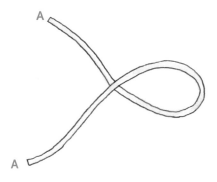

1 Tape the ends of each length of cord to stop them from fraying. Using the cream cord (A), position it as shown above.

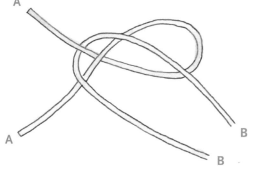

2 Using the picture as a guide, thread the second cream cord (B) through the first.

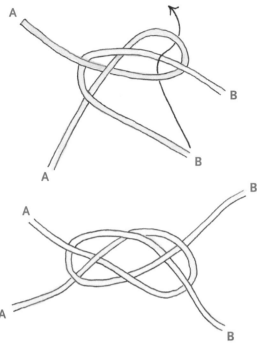

3 Bring the bottom right-hand cord under, over, and then under the other threads. Then tighten the threads to form a knot.

4 Using the blue cord, follow the threading pattern of the first cord so that the blue cord matches the cream cord. Repeat with the second blue cord.

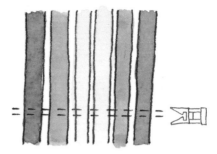

5 Repeat a final time with the red cords to complete your knot.

6 Trim the ends of the cords. For a slightly off-center headband, trim one side of the headband to 6 in (15 cm) and the other to 8 in (20 cm). Stitch the cords together with a straight stitch on the sewing machine, or with a couple of rows of small running stitches.

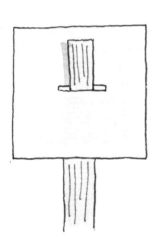

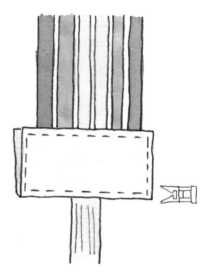

7 Fold the felt squares in half, open them out again and cut a small slit in the center of each with scissors. These should be just wide enough for the elastic to fit through. Thread the elastic through one of the slits.

8 Place one set of cord ends into the felt, fold over, and stitch around the edge to secure. Repeat with the other end of elastic, felt square, and cord ends to complete your headband.

diagonal striped braids

YOU WILL NEED

Four 36-in (80-cm) lengths of embroidery floss (thread) in each of the following colors: red, cream, light blue, and royal blue

Scissors

Safety pin

Add a nautical striped braid to your wrist to brighten up your clothes. These braids are really cute and can be adapted to suit both boys and girls.

1 Fold the floss in half and tie in a knot to secure. Attach the knot to a pillow with the safety pin. Arrange the threads into the order you want your stripes to appear—we've chosen red, light blue, cream, and royal blue.

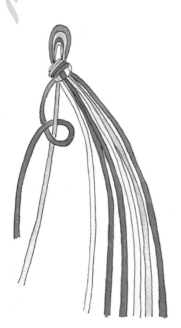

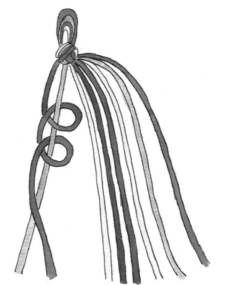

2 Starting with the left-hand floss (red), loop it round the second floss in the sequence to make a half-forward knot (see page 10). Pull the loop tightly to the top of the second floss.

3 Make a second loop in the red floss to complete a forward knot.

4 Repeat steps 2 and 3 in turn on the third, fourth, fifth, sixth, seventh, and eighth lengths of floss, knotting left to right.

further ideas

* Make an irregular striped braid by arranging the floss so some of the colors sit next to each other and others are just a single stripe.

* Why not try making them in your favorite sports team or school colors to show your support?

5 Continue working rows like this with the floss on the left-hand side until your braid is long enough to fit around your wrist, approximately 6 in (15 cm). Tie a knot to secure and trim the ends to 3 in (8 cm).

cross-stitched chains

Jazz up a piece of chain with a few simple stitches for a quick mini project. Try using one, two, or even three pieces of chain.

SKILL LEVEL

YOU WILL NEED

Two 6-in (15-cm) pieces of gold curb chain

Embroidery floss (thread) in blue and red

Needle

Safety pin

Scissors

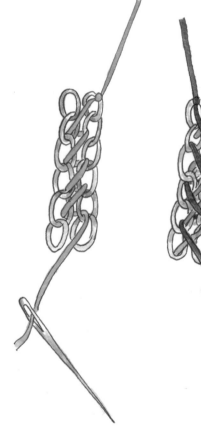

1 Lay the two pieces of gold chain side by side and knot a piece of blue floss to the top link of one chain, leaving a 3-in (8-cm) tail end.

2 Thread the needle with the blue floss and work diagonal stitches over the chains to join them. Once you reach the end of the chains, tie the floss to the end of the second chain and trim to 3 in (8 cm).

3 Then thread the needle with the red floss, knot the floss to the second chain, and work the opposite way over the blue stitches to create cross-stitches. Tie the floss to the end of the first chain and trim the end to 3 in (8 cm).

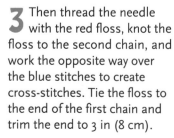

further ideas

* Sew just the edges of one piece of curb chain using white floss—this twists the chain, which looks really pretty.

* Make a wider bracelet by joining three pieces of chain stitched together with diagonal stitches.

alternating square knot braid

Once you've mastered the basic square knot, why not try experimenting with this alternating square knot braid to make wider and more intricate bracelets?

SKILL LEVEL ✿✿

YOU WILL NEED

Four 40-in (1-m) lengths of embroidery floss (threads) in each of the following colors: turquoise, blue, red, and gray

⅛-in (2-mm) silver beads

Safety pin

Scissors

1 Fold your floss in half and tie a knot in the end. Attach it to a pillow with the safety pin.

2 Arrange your threads into the following order: red, turquoise, blue, gray, red, turquoise, blue, and gray.

3 Work a square knot (see page 13) using the first four lengths of floss in the sequence.

89

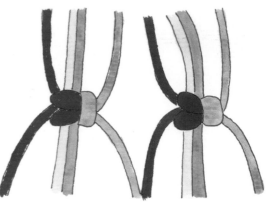

4 Then work another knot using the second set of four lengths of floss.

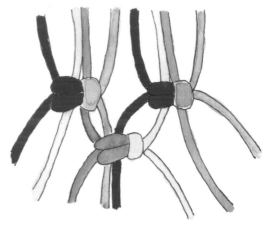

5 For the next square knot you will only use the central four threads—blue, gray, red, and turquoise.

6 Add silver beads to your braid by threading a bead onto both the outside red and outside gray floss before beginning the next row of double square knots.

7 Continue working steps 3–5 until your braid is the desired length, approximately 5 in (12.5 cm).

8 Continue braiding the floss for approximately 3 in (8 cm) and tie in a knot to secure. Trim the ends.

loop charm bracelets

Embellish this loopy bracelet with cute nautical themed charms!

SKILL LEVEL ✿ ✿

YOU WILL NEED

One 40-in (1-m) length of waxed cord in each of the following colors: red, white, navy blue, and turquoise

Three nautical-themed metal charms

Scissors

Safety pin

1 Fold the lengths of cord in half and tie in a knot at the top. Attach it to a pillow with the safety pin.

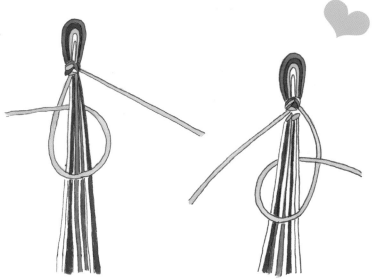

2 Place the turquoise cord either side of the other threads; the remaining cords will become the "core" threads to the bracelet.

3 Make a half-forward knot (see page 10) with the left-hand cord, then a half-backward knot with the right-hand cord. Repeat these two knots eight times.

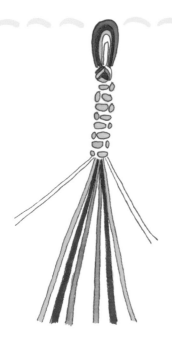
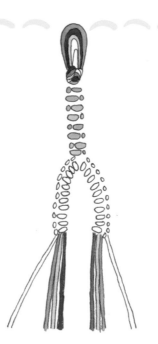
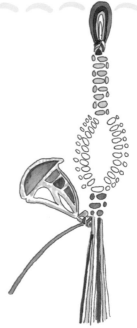

4 Place the white cord either side of the core threads (the turquoise cords now move into the "core" bunch of threads). Divide the core in two so there is 1 x turquoise, 1 x red, and 1 x navy cord in each bunch.

5 Work 10 half-forward knots on the left-hand bunch with the white cord, and then work 10 half-backward knots on the right-hand bunch with the other white cord.

6 Then repeat steps 2–5 with the navy and red cords, but remember to thread a charm onto the braiding cord when you are halfway through a straight section. Repeat this until you have three loops and three charms in place. Finish with the turquoise cord that you started with.

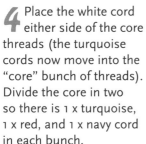

further ideas

* Combine the loops with braiding to make a simpler bracelet. Tie six pieces of cord together (2 x 3 colors) and braid them for 2 in (5 cm), then work loops as described in step 5, but instead of having a straight section in-between the loops, just switch the colors around and repeat step 5 again. Finish with another 2 in (5 cm) section of braiding.

7 Tie a knot to finish and trim the ends to 3 in (8 cm).

bar links bracelet

Create this sleek looking fashionable metal links bracelet using simple knots and nylon cord. Try making it in different colors for each of your friends.

SKILL LEVEL ✿✿

YOU WILL NEED

One 40-in (1-m) length of nylon cord in both blue and cream

Two 40-in (1-m) lengths of nylon cord in red

Safety pin

30 silver bar links

Scissors

1 Tie a knot at the end of the cords and attach it to a pillow using the safety pin.

B C A D

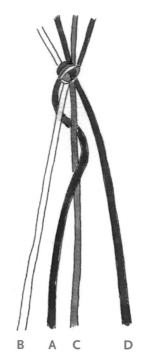

B A C D

B A D C

2 Arrange your cords into the following order—red (A), white (B), blue (C), and red (D). Move cord A under cords B and C.

3 Then move cord A over cord C so the order is now white (B), red (A), blue (C), and red (D).

4 Then repeat on the right-hand side with cord D, moving it under cords C and A, and then over cord A. The order is now white (B), red (A), red (D), and blue (C).

5 Repeat steps 2–4, taking the left-hand cord under the two middle cords and over one cord to the right, then the right-hand cord under the two middle cords and over one cord to the left. So cord B moves under cords A and D and then back over cord D, then cord C moves under cords D and B and then back over cord B, and so on. Do this until your cord measures 3 in (8 cm).

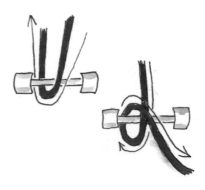

6 Now start knotting the bars in place. The knots are made on the underside of the bars; these will look like crosses. On the front of the bracelet, the knots will be smooth and even. Take the left-hand red cord and wrap it over and under the bar. Then wrap it back over the bar to the left of the first wrap.

7 Wrap the cord under the bar to the right of the first loop, then pull it through the cross loop to tighten.

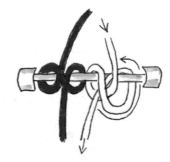

8 The knots for the other three cords are worked slightly differently. Take the next cord and wrap it over and under as before, but then pull it through the first loop (rather than the cross loop) to position it to the left. Repeat step 8 for the other two cords.

9 Add the rest of the bars in the same way before braiding a further 3 in (8 cm) of cord as explained in steps 2–4. Tie a knot and trim the ends to complete.

This cord is so easy to make, just twist and twist and twist some more! Then attach a cool anchor charm to add to the nautical theme.

twisted cord anchor bracelet

SKILL LEVEL ✿

YOU WILL NEED

One 120-in (3-m) length of nylon cord in each of the following colors: red, white, and blue

Safety pin

1 in (2.5 cm) silver anchor charm

Scissors

1 Fold the cord in half, tie a knot, and attach it to a pillow with the safety pin.

2 Hook the cord on your finger and begin to twist. Continue until the twists are so tight that the cord begins to fold up on itself.

3 Thread on the anchor charm and push it to the center of the cord, making sure you keep hold of the cord so that it doesn't unravel.

4 Fold the twisted cord in half, allowing it to twist onto itself, creating one twisted cord.

5 Take the end of the cord and tie it just above where the anchor charm is attached to complete the bracelet. The knot should slide up and down over the nylon cord to allow the bracelet to be adjustable. You can also wrap the loose charm end of the bracelet around the main bracelet to shorten it.

nautical knots

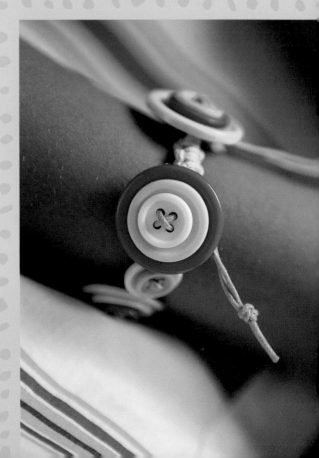

CHAPTER 4
neon brights

Diamond braid bracelet • Shoelace bracelets
Picture bead bracelets • Wrapped bangles • Button bracelets
Joined zigzag bracelet • Braided headphones
Four-strand round cords

diamond braid bracelet

A chunky braided bracelet for the more advanced crafter! Use your skills learned in earlier projects to make this really cool and bright chunky braid with chain detail. It's perfect for livening up an outfit.

SKILL LEVEL ✿✿✿

YOU WILL NEED

One 80-in (2-m) length of embroidery floss (thread) in each of the following colors: pink, yellow, turquoise, purple, orange, and fluorescent green

Safety pin

Scissors

Needle

Two 6-in (15-cm) pieces of gold curb chain

1 Begin by folding the six lengths of floss in half and tying them in a knot. Attach the loop to a pillow with the safety pin.

2 Arrange your floss into the following order—pink, yellow, turquoise, purple, orange, fluorescent green, fluorescent green, orange, purple, turquoise, yellow, and pink.

3 Begin braiding as you did with the chevron bracelet (see page 26), working from the left outside pink thread to the center using forward knots (see page 10). Then work backward knots (see page 10) with the right-hand pink thread to the center. Tie the two pink lengths of floss together using a forward knot. Repeat this with the yellow, turquoise, and purple floss.

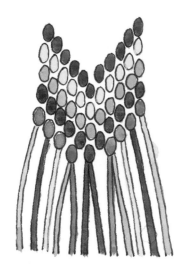

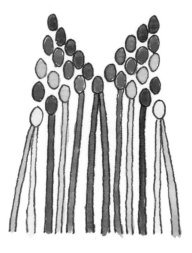

4 Take the left-hand orange floss and work four forward knots only and then four backward knots with the right-hand orange floss. Then take the green floss and work three knots each side, then two with the pink, and one with the yellow.

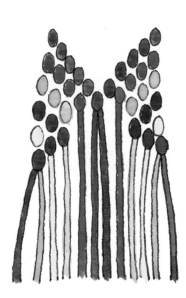

5 Now take the pink left-hand floss and work three backward knots back to the edge of the braid—the first knot is worked over the green floss. Take the right-hand pink floss and work three forward knots to the edge of the braid, again with the first knot being worked over the green floss.

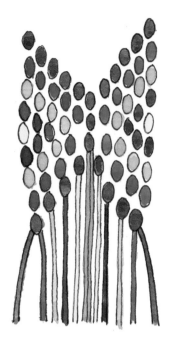

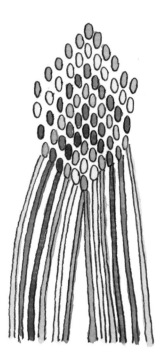

6 Repeat this with the green, orange, and purple floss—so you will make four knots with the green, five with the orange, and six with the purple—and you will finish with an inverted "V" shape.

7 Work four rows of reverse chevron stripe (using backward knots on the left and forward knots on the right of the braid). Then on the next orange row work only five knots on each side; with the purple four knots; the turquoise three knots; the yellow two knots; and the pink one knot.

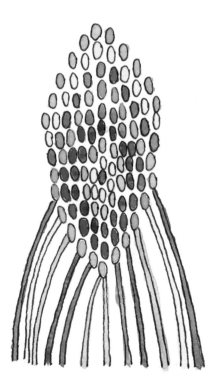

8 Now take the yellow floss and work one forward knot on the left side and one backward knot on the right side. Tie the two lengths of yellow floss together with a forward knot. Repeat with the other lengths of floss until the diamond is complete.

9 Repeat steps 3–9 until your braid is the correct size for your wrist. Tie the lengths of floss into a knot and trim to 3 in (8 cm). Thread the needle with pink floss and stitch a piece of gold curb chain to both sides of the braid.

shoelace bracelets

Shoelaces aren't just for shoes. Try making these really funky bracelets and you will really stand out from the crowd. Why not make some for your friends and start a trend?

SKILL LEVEL ✿✿

YOU WILL NEED

40-in (1-m) length of shoelace

Scissors

Sticky tape

1 Loop the end of the shoelace over itself as shown.

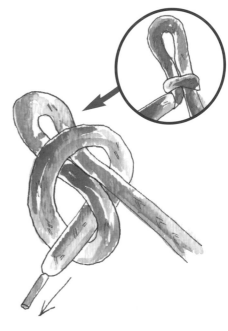

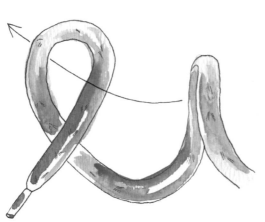

2 Then fold a loop into the long piece of shoelace. Thread it through the first loop you made.

3 Pull the short end of the shoelace to tighten the knot created.

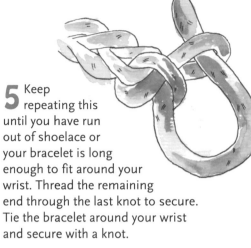

4 Repeat step 2 and thread another loop through the first one. Holding onto the loop you've just threaded (it might be helpful to hook it onto your finger), pull both ends of the shoelace to tighten the next knot.

5 Keep repeating this until you have run out of shoelace or your bracelet is long enough to fit around your wrist. Thread the remaining end through the last knot to secure. Tie the bracelet around your wrist and secure with a knot.

If your shoelace needs trimming because it is too long when you finish braiding, cut a small piece of sticky tape and wind it tightly around the end of the lace. Then cut the lace at the end of the sticky tape and it shouldn't fray. Tie the bracelet around your wrist and secure with a knot.

Instead of making pictures with beads, why not make a cool bracelet? Layer them up on your wrist, and mix and match with thicker and thinner designs.

picture bead bracelets

SKILL LEVEL

YOU WILL NEED

Two 20-in (50-cm) lengths of embroidery floss (thread) in fluorescent colors

Safety pin

Brightly colored picture beads (Hama beads)

Needle

Scissors

1 Knot the two lengths of floss together, about 3 in (8 cm) from the top. Using a safety pin, attach the knot to a pillow.

2 Thread 32 picture beads onto one of the lengths of floss (A) to make a pattern.

A   B

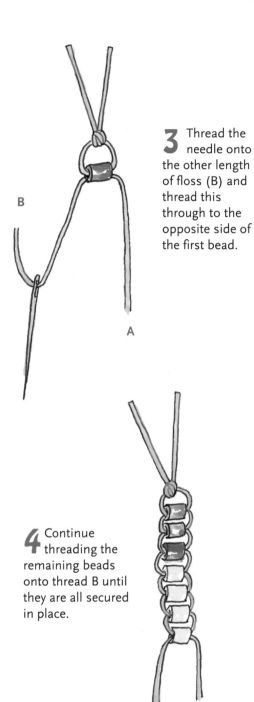

3 Thread the needle onto the other length of floss (B) and thread this through to the opposite side of the first bead.

B

A

4 Continue threading the remaining beads onto thread B until they are all secured in place.

5 Tie a knot after the last bead and trim the floss to 3 in (8 cm).

further ideas

* Create a wider bracelet, or choker, by threading the floss through three beads at a time. You will need to thread 96 beads in step 2.

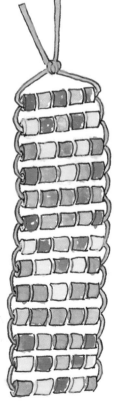

* Create a chevron pattern by following the beading pattern shown here. It may be easier with this design to thread the first row onto thread A and then fix it in place with thread B before moving onto the next row, so the pattern stays correct.

These bangles are so bright and colorful yet so simple to make you will end up with an armful in no time! Try experimenting with what you wrap round your bangle.

wrapped bangles

SKILL LEVEL ✿

YOU WILL NEED

Rhinestone trim

Plastic orange or red bangles

Glue

Scissors

Embroidery floss (thread) in yellow, pink, orange, and fluorescent green

Needle

Fluorescent green shoelace

Pink yarn

Lime green pompom trim

1 Cut a piece of rhinestone chain the same size as the circumference of one of your bangles. Glue it to the center of the bangle, ensuring no glue shows. Let dry.

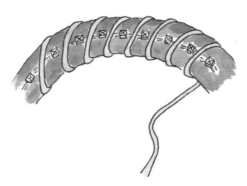

2 Cut a piece of yellow floss 24 in (60 cm) long. Wrap it around the bangle, positioning the floss in between each rhinestone, and tie in a tight knot once you've covered the whole thing.

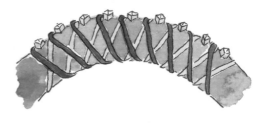

3 Take the pink floss and wrap it around the bangle in the opposite direction to create a criss-cross effect.

4 Tie the two ends of the floss together and, using a needle, thread both this and the fluorescent yellow floss through the inside threads of the bangle to secure. Trim the ends.

further ideas

* For extra color, stick a fluorescent shoelace around the bangle before gluing on the rhinestone trim.

* Use more than two colors of fluorescent floss—for example, green, pink, yellow, and orange—and wrap them round the bangle twice rather than once.

* Cut a piece of pompom trim the same size as the circumference of your bangle and stick it around the center of the bangle with glue. Cut a 40-in (1-m) piece of pink yarn and wrap it tightly around the bangle, flattening down the strings of the pompom as you work. Once you get back to the start, tie a knot and thread the ends through the back of the wrapping using a needle. Trim the end.

button bracelets

Buttons have never looked so bright and beautiful—layer your favorite buttons, stitch them together, and finish with a clever adjustable macramé fastener.

SKILL LEVEL

YOU WILL NEED

Two 12-in (30-cm) pieces of waxed cord in turquoise

One 12-in (30-cm) piece of waxed cord in yellow

Assorted plastic buttons—five large, nine medium, and nine small

Scissors

1 Arrange your buttons into nine piles, five with three buttons layered up, and four with two buttons on top of each other.

2 Take one of the turquoise cords and thread it through the diagonally facing holes on each pile of buttons.

3 Then take the second turquoise cord and thread it through the remaining diagonal holes. Push the buttons close together along the cords so they sit snugly.

4 Fold the yellow waxed cord in half and make a lark's head knot (see page 11) over the four ends of the button bracelet.

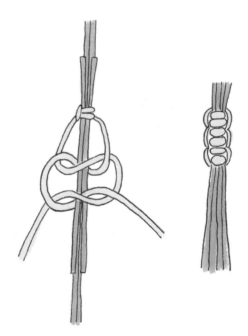

5 Work six square knots (see page 13) over the four turquoise cords. Pull tight to secure, then tie the yellow cords in a tight knot and thread them back into the knot. Trim as short as possible. Tie both sets of short turquoise ends into knots to complete.

neon brights

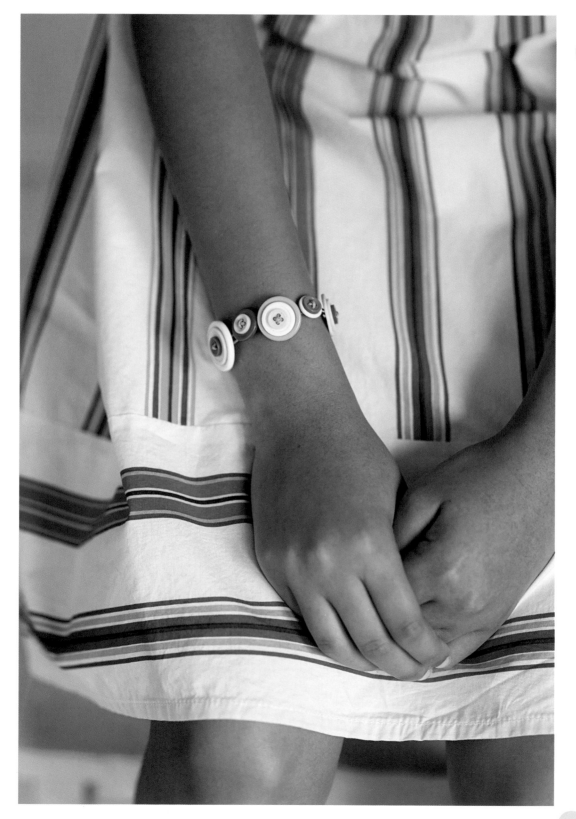

joined zigzag bracelet

You'll be zigzagging all over the place with this bright and zingy macramé braid! Try making single zigzag braids by repeating steps 3 and 4 only if you require a narrower or quicker-to-make bracelet.

SKILL LEVEL ✿✿

YOU WILL NEED

One 60-in (1.5-m) length of embroidery floss (thread) in each of the following colors: cream, turquoise, fluorescent pink, green, and purple

Safety pin

Assorted small beads

Scissors

1 Fold the floss in half and tie in a knot at the top. Attach it to a pillow with the safety pin.

2 Arrange your floss into the following order— cream, turquoise, pink, green, purple, purple, green, pink, turquoise, and cream.

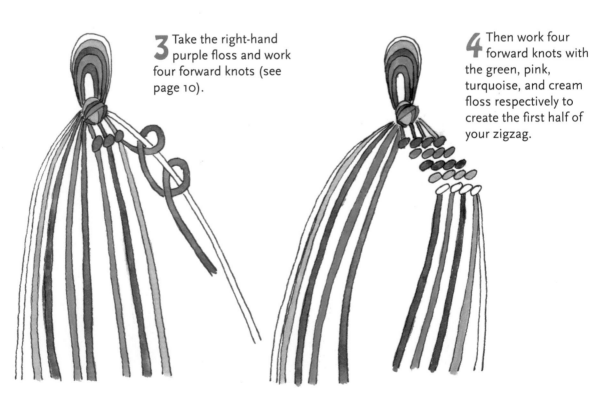

3 Take the right-hand purple floss and work four forward knots (see page 10).

4 Then work four forward knots with the green, pink, turquoise, and cream floss respectively to create the first half of your zigzag.

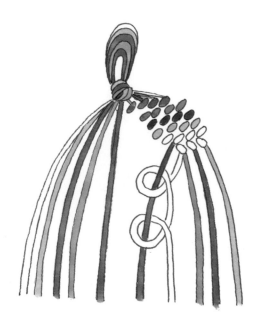

5 Now work the braid in the opposite direction. Take the cream floss you have just used and work four backward knots (see page 10).

6 In the same way, work four backward knots with the turquoise, pink, green, and purple floss.

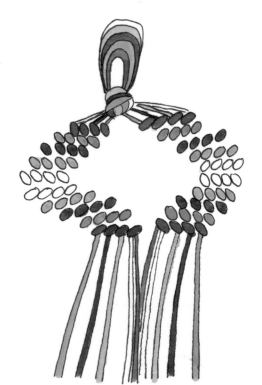

7 Repeat steps 3 and 4 in reverse with the left-hand threads. Starting with the purple floss, work four backward knots. Repeat with the green, pink, turquoise, and cream floss. Then work four forward knots with the turquoise, pink, green, and purple floss.

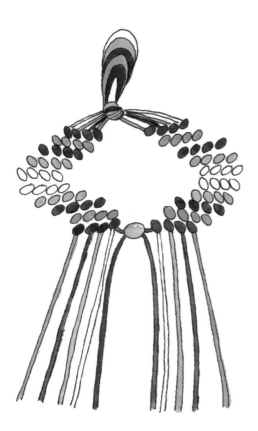

8 To join the zigzags together, thread the left-hand central purple floss through the left side of a bead and the right-hand central purple floss through the right side of the bead so that they cross over.

9 Repeat steps 3–8 until your braid measures approximately 6 in (15 cm). Tie a knot and trim the ends to 3 in (8 cm).

These braided headphones will look as cool as the music you're listening to, using a simple, spiral braid to cover the wires.

braided headphones

SKILL LEVEL ❀

YOU WILL NEED

Two 60-in (1.5-m) lengths of embroidery floss (thread) in each of the following colors: green, orange, blue, purple, and fluorescent yellow

Headphones

Needle

Scissors

1 Arrange your floss into two sets so that one of each color is in each set. Knot the ends of one of the sets of floss onto one of the earpiece wires.

2 Starting with the yellow floss, make a half-forward knot (see page 10) around the other working threads, the thread ends leading from the knot, and the headphone wire.

3 Pull the knot tight and move gently up to the top of the wire.

4 Continue with 11 more yellow half-forward knots. These will twist to create a spiral pattern.

5 Change to purple floss and work 12 more knots. Repeat with the blue, orange, and green floss until the entire wire is covered. Trim the base threads and, using a needle, thread the last knotting floss up through the braid to secure. Trim the ends.

6 Repeat on the second earpiece wire.

four-strand round cords

Delicate round cords look great worn alone or braided together to create a chunkier bracelet.

SKILL LEVEL ✿✿

YOU WILL NEED

One 40-in (1-m) length of embroidery floss (thread) in both fluorescent yellow and pink

Safety pin

Scissors

1 Fold the lengths of floss in half and tie a knot in the top. Attach the loop to a pillow using the safety pin.

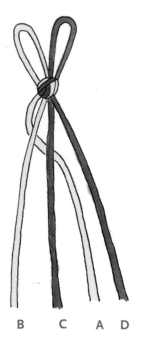

B C A D

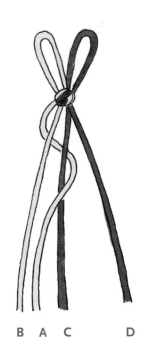

B A C D

B

A D C

2 Arrange your floss into the following order— yellow (A), yellow (B), pink (C), and pink (D). Move floss A under floss B and C.

3 Next, move floss A over floss C.

4 Repeat this wrapping process on the right-hand side using floss D. Move it under floss C and A, and then over floss A.

5 Repeat steps 2–4 until your braid fits around your wrist. Tie a knot and trim the ends to 3 in (8 cm).

further ideas

* To make a thicker bracelet, use six 40-in (1-m) lengths of embroidery floss (thread) in each of the following colors: pink, yellow, orange, purple, jade green, and lime. Fold the threads in half and tie in a knot. Divide them into three bunches of four—yellow/purple, jade/orange and pink/lime. Work the braids following steps 2–4, until they measure approximately 8 in (20 cm) long. Tie a loose knot at the end of each to keep them together. Then braid (plait) them together to form one large braid and tie in a knot at the bottom. Trim the ends.

templates

Braiding Wheel
Bracelets page 32

STRIPES

FLOWERS

HEARTS

DIAMONDS

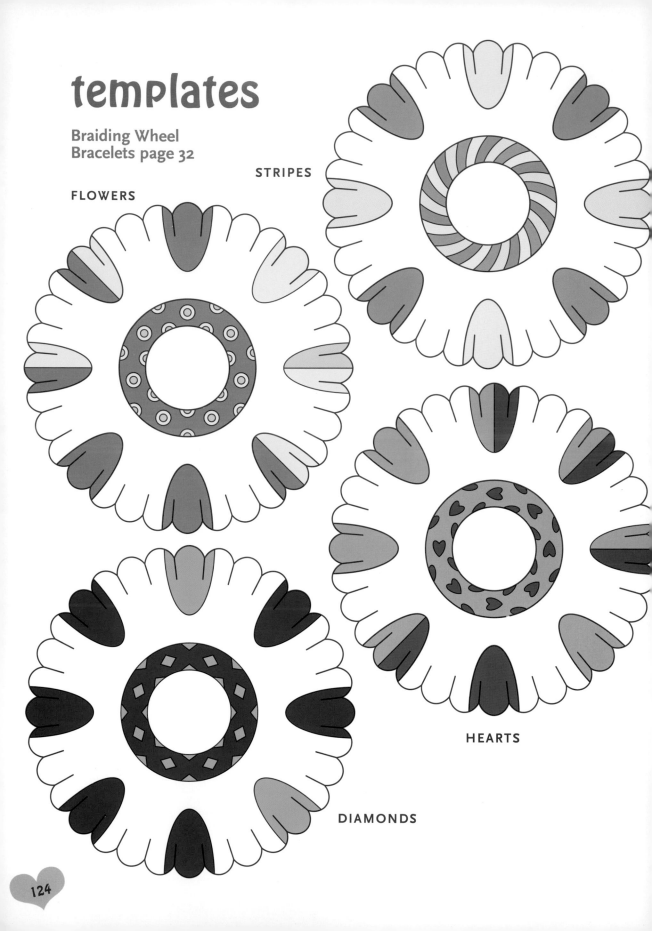

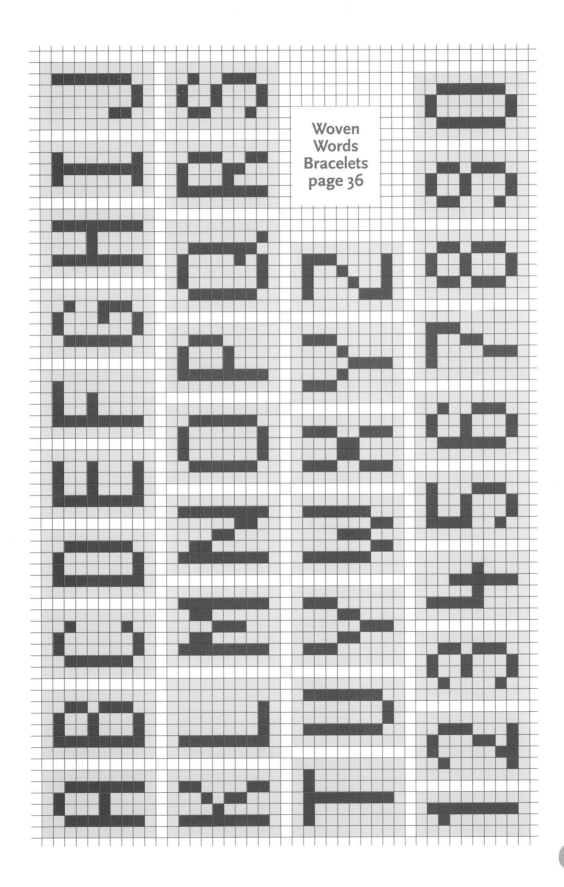

Woven
Words
Bracelets
page 36

suppliers

NORTH AMERICA

A.C. Moore
www.acmoore.com

Britex Fabrics
www.britexfabrics.com

Buy Fabrics
www.buyfabrics.com

Discount Fabrics USA
www.discountfabricsusacorp.com

Fabricland
www.fabricland.com

J & O Fabrics
www.jandofabrics.com

Hobby Lobby
www.hobbylobby.com

Jo-Ann Fabric and Craft Store
www.joann.com

Michaels
www.michaels.com

Purl Patchwork
www.purlsoho.com

The Charm Factory
www.charmfactory.com

ALEX Toys
www.alextoys.com

Ace Hardware
www.acehardware.com

UK

Abakhan Fabrics
www.abakhan.co.uk

Coats Crafts
www.coatscrafts.co.uk

Hobby Craft
www.hobbycraft.co.uk

John Lewis
www.johnlewis.com

Kleins
www.kleins.co.uk

Liberty
www.liberty.co.uk

Rowan Yarns
www.knitrowan.com

The Great Big Bead Shop
www.thegreatbigbeadshop.co.uk

Beads Direct Ltd
www.beadsdirect.co.uk

Josy Rose
www.josyrose.com

Homebase
www.homebase.co.uk

index

acknowledgments

Firstly, I would like to thank all at CICO for yet another fantastic crafting title! You have been a pleasure to work with—the book looks amazing. Special mention must go to Carmel, Katharine, and Louise for all the intricate knot based emails that have taken place over the last few months! I could not have done it without you.

I must also thank my fireman Jamie for his constant support, encouragement, and acceptance of all the crafting paraphernalia scattered around our flat. He also made me the happiest girl in the world by asking me to marry him during the writing of this book— I can't wait to become your Mrs G!